How to Launch Your Career *in* TV NEWS

How to Launch Your Career *in* TV NEWS

Jeff Leshay

VGM Career Horizons
a division of *NTC Publishing Group*
Lincolnwood, Illinois USA

Cover Photo Credits:
Upper right and lower
left, NASA; lower right,
WGN Television.

Library of Congress Cataloging-in-Publication Data

Leshay, Jeff.
    How to launch your career in TV news / by Jeff Leshay.

    p.   cm.
    ISBN 0-8442-4138-5
    1. Television broadcasting of news—Vocational guidance.
I. Title.
PN4784.T4L37   1993
070.1¾495—dc20   92-40027
                                                    CIP

Published by VGM Career Horizons, a division of NTC Publishing Group.
© 1993 by NTC Publishing Group, 4255 West Touhy Avenue,
Lincolnwood (Chicago), Illinois 60646-1975 U.S.A.
All rights reserved. No part of this book may be reproduced, stored
in a retrieval system, or transmitted in any form or by any means,
electronic, mechanical, photocopying, recording or otherwise, without
the prior permission of NTC Publishing Group.
Manufactured in the United States of America.

3 4 5 6 7 8 9 0 VP 9 8 7 6 5 4 3 2 1

Dedicated to my son, Austin James Leshay,
class of 2012

Contents

Frivolous openings. High impact. Getting attention
creatively. Using just the right shots. Writing to
pictures. The buck stops here. Going live.
Reporters who also want to anchor. The anchor's
tape. The sports reporter's tape. The sports
anchor's tape. The weather tape. The producer's
tape. The right specs. Tapes galore. Laborious
labeling.

About the Author

Jeff Leshay is an independent TV news reporter, producer, and consultant. He recently spent three years with CNBC as a correspondent in New York and Chicago, covering business, consumer, and environmental issues. Mr. Leshay also worked as a reporter and anchor at KRDO-TV in Colorado Springs and KYEL-TV in Yuma, Arizona, where he won nine Associated Press broadcasting awards.

Before becoming a TV news reporter, Mr. Leshay was a writer for The Associated Press. He holds a master of science degree from Northwestern University's Medill School of Journalism and a bachelor of arts degree in history from the University of California, Santa Barbara.

Mr. Leshay competed on the varsity tennis team at U.C.S.B., and spent a few years as a touring and teaching tennis professional. He resides in New York with his wife, Julie, and son, Austin.

Foreword

The best thing to be said about cliches is that they are generally true. And the cliche about the first job in television news being the toughest to get is no exception.

Many factors combined in the late 1980s and early 1990s to tighten the television journalism job market even more than normal. The United States economy slipped slowly into recession. Cable television growth continued steady pressure on over-the-air broadcasting for viewers. Advertising expenditures on television flattened. Inflation slowed advertising rate increases. Profit margins declined.

Cutbacks in the news departments of the major television networks received national publicity. Television stations also reduced their news staffs. And the cliche about first jobs being the toughest to get grew into what I call a "common wisdom." It was: there are no new jobs in television journalism.

Well, that is not true. Or, as we'd say in Waynespeak: "NOT."

Growth in traditional television media hiring has slowed, but not stopped. However, at the same time, new opportunities requiring the same broadcast journalism skills are opening. The most notable example is the steady increase of local, 24-hour-a-day all news cable channels.

Thirty-five years ago, when I started in television news, the career path—and dream—was simple and straight. Small station, large station, larger station, network news division, overseas assignment. Few of us planned—or dreamed—beyond that.

Television news careers today are not limited to television stations. If you look ahead at some of the developments expected by the end of this century, you realize the job market is going to explode. For example:

–Direct broadcast satellite delivery of 100-plus channels to the home may start in the mid-1990s. Will there be news and information programming? Of course.

–The regional Bell operating companies are slowly being freed of federal regulation so they can go into the video delivery business, and maybe eventually program production and ownership. Will they deliver news and information programming? Of course.

–When optical fiber to the home and video compression techniques dramatically increase the number of channels on our new high definition television sets to 1000 or maybe 2000, will there be increased need for news and information programming? Of course.

The editorial process we call journalism today more than ever needs skilled, dedicated, hard-working, intelligent young people who believe an informed citizenry is the basis of our democracy.

News does not gather itself. Nor does it automatically arrange itself into programs. That's what reporters, writers, editors and producers do.

These days, jet planes and satellites make it relatively easy to place a reporter and a camera at a news event anyplace in the world. And it is also easy to give that reporter the ability to go "live" the moment he or she arrives at the story. But the reporter must have something to say. That's why television news today needs people who can report, think, analyze, make judgments and speak intelligently into a microphone almost at the same time.

It is exciting. But it is not as easy as it looks.

Regretfully, television journalism is seen by many "wannabes" as a glamour business. And to some it can and will become only that. "Face time"—a phrase I hate—is the career goal of many. These are the people who just want to be on television. The concept of having something intelligent to say once "on" excapes them.

Years ago, I was producing an election night broadcast on NBC. Seconds before our main anchor, David Brinkley, switched to veteran newsman Frank McGee for a report on the Congressional races, our computers went down. McGee had no new vote results. So he analyzed everything that had happened to that minute and when the numbers appeared before him, wove them into what he was saying. All without a script. Frank

McGee knew his subject. And that night on live television, it showed.

There is glamour and excitement in television news. Whether in front of the camera or behind it in the newsroom, it comes from reporting a story better than anyone else, from writing a script faster, producing a program with more insight—from doing the job.

Writing, reporting and editing are the basics, but operating a newsroom computer is becoming mandatory. Knowing how to shoot and edit news video tape is important along with graphics design ability. Today's complete television journalist can do all that.

The first job *is* difficult to acquire. The cliche is true. It always has been difficult. But that has never stopped good people from getting their first job.

This book by Jeff Leshay will help young journalists understand the process as they begin their career in television news. Mr. Leshay's advice is solid, practical and realistic.

Robert Mulholland
Director of Broadcast News
Programs at Northwestern University
and former president of NBC

Introduction

During the 1991 Miss America Pageant, a dozen of the candidates announced on national television that they wanted to be TV news anchors, reporters, or sportscasters. It was truly an embarrassing moment for some of us in the television news business who take our jobs very seriously. Not that there's anything wrong with intelligent, attractive people wanting to become TV journalists. It was the reasons a few of the women gave that made me uncomfortable.

Miss Illinois, for example, who had appeared in the television series "Growing Pains," proudly stated that she planned to combine her acting skills with her interest in journalism. Actress Barbara Eden, who was cohosting the show, quickly added that Miss Illinois would do very well as a newscaster because she had already had TV experience.

Indeed, TV anchors and reporters, some more than others, employ a bit of acting in their work, to maximize the effectiveness of stories. And many who make it to the top of the profession are attractive people, or at least not unpleasant to look at. But the most important skills TV journalists bring to the newsroom, whether they work on- or off-camera, have little to do with appearance. They must be able to quickly gather information from a variety of sources, pinpoint the most important issues, and then deliver the news to the viewing audience succinctly, simply, and smoothly.

A combination of glamour and journalistic purpose is drawing thousands of people each year into TV news. The competition is fierce for a limited number of jobs. This book describes the positions in news, weather, and sports and tells you how to go about finding them. It includes the insight and advice of some of America's best-known TV news veterans and others still paying their dues at small TV stations in small towns.

Whether you're still in school, fresh out of school, or making a major career change, this book will help you determine whether TV news is the right career for you, and if so, where you'll best fit in. Once you've made those decisions, it'll give you a competitive edge in the job search and help you launch a successful career in electronic journalism.

You'll find that *persistence*, often mentioned in this book, is the key to finding internships and paid positions in TV news, and then maximizing your performance on-camera or behind the scenes once you've broken in. Neither task is easy. But TV news is a business in which persistence and old-fashioned hard work, often on weekends and holidays when your friends are vacationing, really do pay off. Few TV journalists grow rich, but the nonmonetary returns are great. No other business is as exciting day in and day out. Each day poses a new set of rewarding challenges.

In 1987 I left my job as a newswriter with the Associated Press to pound the pavement looking for my first on-camera reporter job. I had also worked briefly for the Financial News Network and attended the graduate broadcast journalism program at Northwestern University. The instructors at Northwestern's Medill School of Journalism, drawing from many years of experience in the "real world," taught us a great deal about putting together TV news stories, and how to use those skills to find jobs.

As various job possibilities arose, however, I found that each one offered a unique set of circumstances. So I called my former instructors periodically for advice. They were kind enough to counsel me on the tailoring of application materials, including resumes, cover letters, and audition tapes, for specific jobs at TV stations. I took many pages of notes on their advice, and on sporadic job-hunting tips and leads I found in various trade publications.

After finding next to nothing on the subject in bookstores and libraries, I began to realize there was no single comprehensive set of job-hunting guidelines specifically geared for people looking to build a career in the highly competitive TV news field.

While working in my first two TV news reporter jobs in Yuma, Arizona, and Colorado Springs, Colorado, I received a lot of phone calls from other graduates of the Medill program and friends of friends inquiring about job possibilities. I spent a lot of time on the phone with aspiring TV journalists sharing my own experiences and much of the advice I had collected from others.

After a lengthy phone conversation one night with one recent graduate about his application materials, my wife suggested it would be a lot easier to write down all the advice I was giving and the names of other resources that might prove helpful. Out of that writing grew this book.

Given the popularity of TV news, I couldn't believe so little had been written detailing the various positions in TV newsrooms and precisely how to go about landing one of those jobs. A photographer friend of mine suggested that's because everyone in the business is so busy trying to succeed that no one has had time to write such a book!

Through my own research and job searches I had learned much about the likes and dislikes of those who do the hiring at TV stations. I had often dreamed of writing a book, though not necessarily on the subject at hand, and this seemed like the perfect opportunity. Knowing how rewarding a career in TV news can be, the writing of this book and the chance to help others break into the business became a labor of love.

Other publications, some of which I refer to, do a wonderful job focusing specifically on TV newswriting, reporting, editing, photography, and other skills required in putting together powerful newscasts. This book, too, examines those issues, but within the context of utilizing such skills to land that first job and build the framework for a successful career.

There are valid arguments that television news isn't always what it should be—that TV stations often spend their money building aesthetically pleasing sets and hiring anchors with pretty faces instead of focusing their attention on journalistic values. TV news is, after all, a business much like many others. Commercial TV stations must make money to stay in business, and that means attracting viewers and advertising revenues.

The methods by which TV news operations are run have been and will undoubtedly continue to be the subject of debate for many years to come. Many stations have cut back on expenses to improve their troubled bottom lines, and some TV news critics and employees complain—and justifiably so—that at many stations the goal of maintaining healthy profits outweighs the goal of producing important, informative stories that require an investment of more time and money. The kinds of stories they're referring to are those that keep in check the powerful groups, in the public and private sectors, that make our society tick. Many such stories, critics argue, go untold.

But there's no doubt that the potential of television as a news medium is incredibly vast. And when done right, it's a wonderful resource for information. TV news can provide an incredible aural and visual experience that takes viewers to the scenes of important stories and allows them to draw conclusions of their own.

To be involved in TV news that only seeks to fill a half hour with lots of color and little substance can be frustrating. To do it right requires a seemingly endless supply of energy and dedication, and the desire to return to work the next day and do it all again with a whole new set of stories.

TV newsrooms are filled with dynamic personalities. And even under a tremendous amount of deadline pressure, the teamwork is fun. Together, you witness history in the making and open viewers' eyes to what's happening in the world and how those events might affect them. The job is incredibly important, rewarding, and influential. I can think of no more worthwhile career.

I thank Professor Vernon Stone of the University of Missouri, who has spent many years conducting valuable research for the Radio-Television News Directors Association, and some of whose data and insight I've included in this book.

I also offer special thanks to two of my graduate instructors, Rick Brown in Chicago and Lou Prato in Washington. Each, in his own candid way, provided me with no-holds-barred constructive criticism and advice on how to produce compelling TV news stories, how to use those stories effectively in the search, and what to expect once working in the business. They've been true friends who have continued to provide me with career counseling during the past several years.

Speaking of counseling, I'd be remiss, and perhaps in a bit of trouble, if I didn't thank my parents for their constant friendship and support through the years.

Last, but far from least, I thank my wife, Julie, for her endless understanding and encouragement during the long hours I've spent working in TV news, and the other long hours I've spent writing this book. She has demonstrated the value of having a partner in life who supports you every step of the way. And in the highly volatile TV news business, that may be your single most valuable asset.

■1■
What's It
All About?

On-camera and behind the scenes, television news is providing more opportunities than ever for careers packed with thrills and rewards. The profession, though it receives and deserves a healthy dose of criticism, is a noble one. Electronic journalism combines the information-gathering skills of journalists and photographers with state-of-the-art technology to quickly shed light on the world's increasingly complex problems and how they affect our lives. At its best television news makes sense out of those issues by focusing on the most critical points. The challenge is to do so in a relatively short period of time, yet without oversimplifying, which can be just as dangerous as not communicating the information at all.

Each day TV news teams must overcome nerve-racking obstacles to gather as much information as possible on the stories being covered. The process is highly rewarding when the important details of those stories are conveyed to the viewers. What makes television news even more exciting are the microwave, fiber-optic, and satellite technologies that allow TV journalists to report information live, whether from around the block or halfway around the planet. CNN greatly enhanced its reputation in 1991 by committing an unprecedented amount of resources to live coverage of the Persian Gulf War.

Responding to a Thirst for Knowledge

Time constraints in television newscasts sometimes prevent the depth and analysis one might find in a newspaper or newsmagazine. Such periodicals can devote more words, perspective, and hindsight to a subject. But viewers' insatiable thirst for knowledge about the world in which we live and the rapid growth of the cable TV industry have paved the way for more, and more informative, local and national TV news and magazine-format shows than ever.

"What I perceive as growing is the appetite for news and information, particularly if you define that very, very broadly, recognizing that this offends the traditional journalist," says Marv Rockford, award-winning news director at NBC's KCNC-TV in Denver. "But if you look at not only programs like local news broadcasts, or network broadcasts, or CNN broadcasts, but you look at 'Entertainment Tonight,' 'Current Affair,' all of these tabloid-type shows, they're all information, reality-based shows. Your values are different in each show, but the skills you use to put on those shows are all basically the same. It's just a question of how you apply those skills.

"So the fact is the market for what we do is expanding, not constricting," Rockford continues. "And what we're going to find is that more and more people will be working in what I guess you would call traditional television news department environments. I wouldn't dissuade anybody from getting into the business because he or she thinks there's a lack of opportunity. Regional sports channels, for example, are growing—little, mini–ESPN-type stations, targeted at specific regions. So there are a lot of opportunities to use the kind of skills we have in this business."

The Well-informed TV Journalist as Educator

The growing demand for information programming means TV journalists must be prepared to quickly cover a great variety of issues, from sports to weather, from agriculture to space symposiums, from city politics to foreign policy. Such preparation entails constant reading while keeping an eye on the tube and an ear at the radio.

"From my perspective, reading is by far the most important thing in this business," says correspondent Cokie Roberts, who covers Washington, DC, for both ABC News and National Public Radio. "You've got to know what's going on in the world. It's absolutely essential."

The more a TV journalist knows about an issue, the easier it is to quickly combine words, pictures, and natural sound to do what print journalists cannot—allow the viewers to actually see and hear events going on around the world. The impact can be enormous. The war in Vietnam remains one of the best examples. Projecting the horrifying sights and sounds of war into American living rooms fueled much of the public opposition that eventually forced the U.S. withdrawal of troops from that country.

The best TV reporters and producers let stories with compelling pictures and sound speak for themselves. They provide some background and news analysis but use much of their narrative only to link and paraphrase the comments, thoughts, and feelings of those involved.

A good journalist is a good educator, able to take complex issues and explain in layman's terms how they affect our lives.

Assignment editors must be able to select the most important stories and coordinate the type of coverage they deserve. Reporters, writers, and photographers are in charge of covering those stories—gathering and communicating the facts, opinions, and pictures necessary to inform the public. Producers are responsible for making the final selection of stories and presenting them in a most compelling manner. The stories must be exciting to watch, yet easy to digest.

Expecting the Unexpected

As a television journalist you must learn where to go, and who to go to, when information is needed in a hurry. Finding and cultivating reliable sources is crucial. Those of us in the news business live and die by our Rolodexes. Up-to-date names, titles, and phone numbers of contacts can really pay off in the pinch—when stories break.

When the unexpected happens, TV news teams must be willing and ready at any time to drop everything they're doing and shift gears into the more urgent story. The best-laid plans are often interrupted. Ironically those interruptions are what we in the news business thrive on and actually look forward to.

Two months after President George Bush was sworn into office, he visited Colorado Springs, Colorado, to speak to a national group of business leaders. He landed in Air Force One, was whisked off to a hotel, and decided to go for an impromptu jog. I had worked hard to set up an interview at that very moment with ABC correspondent Ann Compton for a story I was doing on how the White House press corps covers the president. But when the president decides to go running, that's a newsworthy priority, especially for a local station in a town that may get only one or two presidential visits each term.

A production coordinator from our station who had volunteered to drive around ABC's field crews was pulling into the parking lot of the luxurious Broadmoor Hotel, only to pass Bush's motorcade driving out. One of the savvy network field producers, who had followed the president around the country and was quite familiar with his routine, exclaimed, "That was the president. He's going jogging! Where's the nearest track?"

Our man Scott knew exactly where the closest track was—Cheyenne Mountain High School—and he whirled the car around in the parking lot and headed in that direction. As soon as the crew arrived at the school, Scott ran to the nearest phone and called our station to let us know the president was jogging around the track with a dozen or so students.

A photographer and I raced to the scene, and ABC and its Colorado Springs affiliate had an exclusive. No other television crews were there to capture the moment, and we were able to include the video a half hour later in our early-evening coverage of the president's arrival.

Ann Compton certainly understood why I'd had to postpone our meeting, and I was able to interview her during some "dead time" before the president's speech that evening. Postponements of interviews and stories are part of the business. Although it's not fun canceling shoots that may have taken quite some time to set up, most people understand that's part of the TV news game. Urgent stories can break at any time.

Fast-Pace Impression

The fast, nonstop pace of television news isn't for everyone. Take it from a girl who, as an eighth-grader in Colorado Springs, shadowed a photographer and me for a day as part of a class project. We covered a couple of stories that weren't the pressing type: A partial solar eclipse as seen from a local observatory by scientists and schoolchildren, and a press conference of the local Economic Development Council. This is the job as seen through her eyes, and written in a thank-you letter to the news department:

"I never could have imagined all the steps that are required to put a story on the news! I was so worn out when I got home I'm amazed I even made it through the day. After seeing how hectic your work day is, I think I'll stick to being a novelist, although you never know!! I could end up back at your station hoping to be your intern. . . . Spending a day in (and out) of your newsroom is an experience I'll never forget!"

Indeed, TV news careers, like no other, are filled with unforgettable experiences. If the daily excitement and importance of electronic journalism appeals to you, read on! TV news just may offer the rewarding career you're looking for.

■ 2 ■
Finding Your Niche in the Newsroom

The following are colorful and candid descriptions of the many challenging on- and off-camera jobs in TV news.

News Reporters

For those of you who are true journalists at heart and want to work on-camera, news reporting in the field is probably where you'll find much of the excitement. Only out on the streets do you have the opportunity to investigate stories from beginning to end, meet and interview interesting people every day, learn about new ideas and issues, and then deliver that information to the public.

THE DAILY CHALLENGE

It's a daily challenge to put together a better, more informative story than your competitors, and to do it fast. In his book *Hold On, Mr. President!* ABC's incomparable veteran correspondent Sam Donaldson describes the task of TV news reporting:

6

"Daily news reporting, whether from the White House or any other beat, does not lend itself to considered, studied, letter-perfect work. . . . The ideal way to produce a television spot-news report is to write the entire script, select the soundbite (a comment from someone involved in the story) and pictures to go with it, time everything, then, with all elements firmly in mind and hand, begin the editing process. But when it's forty-five minutes to deadline, you don't have time to do that. You must begin, not quite sure what you'll include, what you'll leave out, what precisely you're going to say, not even sure of the pictures you have to cover your words since there may not have been time to screen all the videotape. . . .

"The debate over what's important to tell in a limited time can fill hours in the classroom or the seminar hall, but at forty-five minutes to deadline, there can be no debate. . . . If you find it impossible to make up your mind about things, for goodness' sake, don't get into the daily news business."

Reporters often work literally on the run, keeping track of numerous events at the same time, and drafting stories on a small notepad while rushing from one scene to another. At many small-market stations reporters must even shoot their own pictures and record their own sound. Hence the title *reporter-photographer* or *one-man-band*.

And another thing—reporters must learn to eat meals in the news vehicle while speeding from one scene to another without getting indigestion. Photographers tend to drive like maniacs, and there's often little time to stop for lunch.

"It's gotta be cheap, it's gotta be good, and it's gotta be fast," says CNBC photographer Mario Schettino. "Otherwise, we just can't eat there. And that's on good days—when we have time for lunch!"

Once the interviews and other pictures are shot, the reporter dashes back to the station to quickly type up the script, record the narration, or *voicetrack*, and edit the words, pictures, and natural sound together into a *package*, or *wrap*, on tape.

DIGGING DEEP

Most reporters, especially those in small markets, are *general assignment reporters*, covering a full range of issues. At medium and large stations, however, some reporters specialize in covering politics, crime, business, consumer affairs, health, agriculture, features, sports, or other subjects.

All reporting should take an investigative, deep-digging approach. A few large news organizations go so far as to employ special investigative teams, sometimes known as I-teams, to fully explore injustices. But such a commitment is time-consuming, expensive, and not always fruitful. Unfortunately, many stations consider that risk too high and end up only covering more obvious issues.

Even though investigative reporter slots per se are few and far between, aggressive fact-finding remains the best way to build a solid reputation as a news reporter. It's up to you to take the initiative early in your career. Small and medium stations often welcome the extra effort, though you'll probably have to do some of your investigative work on your own time.

"I think they're going to have to work on investigative pieces on top of all the other stories they have to do—in other words, on their own time," says Pam Zekman, a Pulitzer- and Peabody-winning investigative reporter at Chicago's WBBM-TV. "Most stations just don't give you the time you need to do that. But once you have the story, they love to air it."

Uncovering fraud and influence peddling at city hall or looking into businesses that are ripping people off won't just bode well for you at your station—it'll impress prospective employers in bigger markets.

Exposing fraud and sham is indeed popular with the viewers and can be personally rewarding. In my first job as a TV news reporter at KYEL-TV in Yuma, Arizona, I produced and reported occasional "Consumer Watch" stories. Viewers would write to the station complaining about certain local businesses. The news director and I would then single out for investigation those gripes that were most compelling.

One such letter complained about an auto repair shop that had taken scores of people for a ride, failing to properly repair their vehicles, and in some cases leaving the cars downright dangerous. Through our investigation of other complaints made to the Better Business Bureau, and with the help of the city's business licensing department, we found that instead of complying with a court order to make good on the faulty repairs, the owner had quietly sold the business to a couple of his mechanics and hightailed it south of the border to Mexico. The new owners claimed to have had no knowledge of the court order, but the negative publicity in our story forced them to make good on some of their shoddy work. We would have preferred to see the garage shut down, but we did deter a lot of people from doing business there. The "high fives" in the newsroom and small celebration at a local pub after the story aired were definitely in order.

NEWS VERSUS SALES

Not all reporting on fraud, however, is as satisfying. In fact, it can be extremely frustrating, especially in small markets where the station's income depends on advertising from a limited number of businesses, none of which the station can easily afford to alienate.

Another complaint I investigated concerned a golf course that had offered senior citizens a discount during a particular time of the day and then refused to live up to its word—a blatant example of false advertising.

When I spoke with the owner of the golf course on the phone, he admitted that he didn't "give a damn" about the seniors to whom he had appealed in a newspaper ad. I was more than ready to expose this jerk's blatant disregard for good business practices. But it just so happened that our sales team had been trying to convince the man to advertise with our station and had just approached him the week before with a sales pitch.

After arguing with the sales department, which had somehow found out we were working on the story, the issue ended up in the general manager's office. He's a fair man, but one who knows all too well the importance of advertising revenues. He decided to accompany the sales manager over to the golf course, where they pleaded with the owner to take back what he had said to me and make good on his offer to the seniors. In return, they told him, and much to my dismay, the station would not broadcast the story. You'd have to be an idiot to turn that deal down. He didn't. And the story never aired.

Needless to say, I was furious. The deal went against everything I believed in, and I still get ticked off just thinking about it. But I took some consolation when I checked and found that the golf course had made good on its offer to seniors, and I knew there would soon be other important stories to investigate and air.

Those frustrations are fewer and farther between in medium and large markets, where the advertising pool is bigger, and news departments take fewer cues from sales managers.

In Chicago, Pam Zekman says her biggest source of frustration as an investigative reporter "is getting people to go on-camera, particularly when they feel foolish or think they might look foolish. So it can be tough to make it interesting television.

"But the rewards can be great," she quickly adds. "You can really get something done. You can even get reforms or legislation passed to correct a problem."

News Anchors

Many people enter the television news arena as aspiring anchors. A dispro-portionately large number of newcomers want to anchor the evening news, hoping to move up to big markets offering six-figure salaries and a lot of fame. But few make it beyond the small and midsize markets, where almost all of those who want to work on-camera must first pay their dues.

Most anchors start out as reporters, and many of them continue to do some field reporting throughout their careers. On the other hand, some reporters spend some of their time anchoring—on weekends, holidays, and when they're needed to fill in for absent anchors. In other words, anchor and re-porter jobs are not mutually exclusive. Many reporters enjoy anchoring, and many anchors like to get their shoes a little muddy from time to time.

Generally speaking, the smaller the market, the more field reporting and writing anchors do, even those who would prefer merely to read the stories on the air. That's mainly because of the staff limitations and the need to fill half-hour newscasts with as much local news as possible. In fact, many anchors in small markets produce and write entire newscasts themselves.

In medium and large markets, however, the writing tasks of anchors sel-dom extend beyond editing or rewriting material written for them by pro-ducers, reporters, writers, and the wire services.

Anchors are often perceived by the public, sometimes correctly, as little more than actors on the set, reading the news to the viewers and setting the mood for the stories presented by reporters. To combat that public perception, many news directors, even in the top markets, make it a point to send anchors out in the field occasionally to demonstrate their involve-ment in stories. There's no doubt that the best anchors are those who are well-informed about the issues and genuinely interested in conveying that information to the public. That kind of credibility is crucial in winning the respect and trust of viewers.

"For anchors, continuing to report is important because you can get in-volved in a story firsthand and treat it with the care and attention it de-serves," says NBC News anchor Garrick Utley. "Reporting is essential for our interest and growth. It's also essential for public perception. It's im-portant for the public to know we're knowledgeable about what's going on."

DISTINGUISHING YOURSELF

The growing number of cable networks specializing in particular types of information has opened more slots for anchors and reporters with expertise in a variety of fields, from sports to health to travel to politics to business. Some of those people have held jobs in those areas. Others have covered the issues extensively as broadcast or print journalists.

"The audience can tell if you know what you're talking about," says CNBC's Sue Herera, one of the most recognized and respected anchors in the financial news arena. "They're much smarter than we often give them credit for. Knowledge of what you're telling the viewers about is really important. You can't fool the people out there.

"I think you're much more marketable with a specialty. There are a lot of people in the media business, and a lot of them want to be on-camera. One of the ways to rise to the top is to be really good and knowledgeable in a particular area. Cable television has advanced the concept of specialty reporting because it tends to be niche oriented, or topic specific."

Herera has worked as a business anchor and reporter since 1981, when she began her career with the Financial News Network (FNN). Herera had studied journalism in college and interned at a couple of TV stations in Los Angeles. Although she had never worked in the financial world, she made it a point to learn everything she could about business and reporting financial news after landing a job writing copy at FNN. Herera attended seminars on such topics as the futures markets—now one of her specialties—read the financial pages regularly, and developed a network of contacts in the business world whom she constantly tapped for information and insight. She still relies on those contacts.

"Because I follow and report on a lot of markets, I need a lot of sources," says Herera. "I call about 15 to 20 traders a day to find out what's moving the markets at that moment and what they expect will happen. Finding out what's moving the markets is the reporter function. Then, as an anchor, I divulge that information.

"It's very rewarding in cable. Specialty reporting allows you to provide perspective you might not have a chance to provide at a local network affiliate or at the network. You get to give the audience, which tends to be more demanding in business television, some depth, and I enjoy having the ability to really go into topics and explain them at length. You still have the deadline and performance pressures that exist at local stations. But you don't have to worry about 'sweeps' [ratings periods], which often mean bringing down the level of information and becoming more sensational to attract viewers.

"The area I cover is complicated, and as a result, part of my job is to explain things in simple English. So in addition to presenting the news, I try to inform and educate the audience."

SMOOTH DELIVERY

Herera and other anchors, whether in specialty or general news, say the importance of smoothly delivering the news on the air shouldn't be underestimated. There's no denying that the anchor's role as news presenter is crucial to the success of the newscast and the station. Anchors must be able to effectively convey the importance of stories, and they must do so in a conversational, not condescending, manner. Anchors must be able to look into a camera and speak to viewers as if they're chatting with friends. Good anchors make the viewers feel every bit as comfortable as they are.

It takes years to develop strong anchoring skills, and the station's ratings depend on them. When ratings drop, sales often follow suit. The station's highly visible anchors are the easiest to blame, though they may not be the root of the problem. Anchors are often the last hired and the first fired.

"The only thing that gives a local station real identity is its news program, and for better or for worse, the principal factor within that identity, in addition to having a good all-around news product, is the strength and recognizability of the anchors," says Michael Eskridge, a former CNBC president whose Broadcast Management Services group manages several local stations around the country.

Eskridge admits the turnover rate among anchors, especially in small markets, is quite high. But he adds, "It's very frequently true that the stations that do best in news have on-air people, not just anchors, but reporters and sportscasters and weathercasters as well, who've been in the market a long time and have a following. People feel comfortable with them."

News managers and sales staffs often refer to anchors—and reporters, for that matter—as talent. I've always disliked the use of that term in the news business because it equates news with entertainment, or at least can be perceived that way. Not that there's anything wrong with entertainment. But in my mind, associating the two means a loss of credibility for broadcast news. Besides, there are many "talented" people working in newsrooms, and not all of them are reporters and anchors.

FAME VIA WISDOM

There's no doubt that anchors are the most-recognized of the station's staff. Such fame appeals to many people entering the business. But if that's more important to you than the job of informing the viewers about events that affect their lives, you ought to think instead about heading to Hollywood for an acting career. The chances of making it to a big market or the network as an anchor are slim. They're even slimmer for those who don't care much about the mission of TV news and fail to develop solid writing and reporting skills along the way.

For anchors who do care about the mission, *persistence* over the years may well pay off. There are many successful anchors who resemble Ken-and-Barbie dolls but who have developed likable, trustable on-air personalities. Most anchors who make it to the big markets have learned through years of experience to conduct intelligent, insightful interviews, smoothly ad lib when the teleprompter breaks down, coordinate live reports from the field while on-camera in the studio, and develop and write news stories.

Aside from demonstrating those skills, Garrick Utley plays a role on the news management side as well.

"I enjoy helping to develop the entire newscast in meetings with the producers," says Utley. "To conceive of the show and have input on the story selection is exciting, as is the presentation and writing involved."

Utley says he carefully reviews each and every script, substantially rewriting much of the material in a way that's most comfortable for him to read.

"TV news is not just a job of anchoring or reporting. We're going to see a lot more crossbreeding of TV news jobs in the future. It's important to be versatile."

News Producers

Working in the limelight isn't for everyone. Producing newscasts can be every bit as exciting as covering stories in the field. Producers control the editorial and production qualities of entire newscasts. They decide which, and when, stories will run, how long they'll be, and how they'll be presented. They also write some of those stories and the transitions between segments of the newscast.

CALLING THE SHOTS

Successful producers are highly organized, paying close attention to each detail. They mark scripts with precise times and camera shots, clearly communicate to the anchors and other members of the staff any last-second changes that need to be made during a newscast, and all the while stay in contact via phones and two-way radios with crews broadcasting live from the field.

"Making people do what you want them to do because it's important to the show can be the biggest frustration," says Karen Horner, who just a few years ago began her career interning and then producing at KRDO-TV in Colorado Springs before moving into a producer slot at Denver's KWGN-TV. "You've got to convince them that even though they might not like it, the particular work they're doing is worthwhile. I prefer to use the nice instead of arrogant approach. I get more accomplished that way."

Producers also check the spelling of names and accuracy of all other graphics superimposed on the screen during a newscast. And in some small markets they spend a fair amount of time editing videotape.

If you find such challenges attractive, and if you can cope with the pressure of having to add, drop, or change stories literally at the last second as news is breaking, you may be a producer at heart.

PIECING THE PUZZLE

"Producing a whole show every day, in a variety of different ways, can be really exciting," says Horner. "You come into work and you've got all these pieces of a puzzle facing you. Every day's a completely different puzzle, and it's definitely a challenge to solve it in a certain amount of time. There are a lot of different ways to put it together. You work on it all day long, trying out the different possibilities. Then you look at the finished product and see whether you're happy with the end result."

In medium and large markets producers write or rewrite material to be read by anchors, including *voice-overs* (voice-over-pictures, also known as VO's), teases (previews of stories coming up), and introductions and tags (conclusions) to field reports. Producers must be able to recognize similarities in stories and group those pieces together, writing smooth transitions to link them in a way that allows information to flow from one to the other.

WRITING FOR SUCCESS

Early in their careers producers and production assistants should write as much copy as possible. That's the best way to develop strong broadcast writing skills and build an impressive portfolio of writing samples to show news directors in larger markets.

"It's definitely harder for news directors to find good behind-the-scenes people than it is to find reporters and anchors," says Rick Brown, a former Milwaukee news director and manager of the CBS News bureau in Chicago, who now teaches at Northwestern University's Medill School of Journalism. "And once they get into the business, talented producers can move faster to bigger markets."

Some reporters and anchors in small markets become more interested in producing than reporting news, having had to produce many of their own stories and newscasts themselves. Their broad-based experience and refined writing skills make them strong candidates for producer jobs at larger stations.

"Writing skills are so important," says Jodi Fleisig, who recently left a producer job at New York's WABC-TV for the executive producer/ assistant news director post at Atlanta's WSB-TV. "You've got to write the way you speak, in a compelling way that grabs the attention of the viewers. Otherwise, they'll tune you out. And as a producer, you are the editor—in charge of every word that's said."

"The writing needs to be very active," says Karen Horner. "But the most important thing is to make sure your writing makes sense. Don't forget that what we're writing is for people to hear. That's why it's important to proofread the material aloud—to make sure it sounds OK."

AN EYE- AND EAR-OPENING EXPERIENCE

After pounding the pavement for a couple of months, I got my first job in television news at the Los Angeles bureau of the Financial News Network (later acquired by CNBC) as a part-time production coordinator. That was just a glorified title given to those of us who ripped scripts and wire copy for higher-ranking members of the staff, answered the phones, and gathered the latest data from the stock exchanges. I had no keen interest in financial news at the time, but it was a foot in the door.

After a month or so I moved into a full-time slot doing the same tasks. And only a month after that, the news director called me into his office.

"Jeff," he said, "I've got some good news and some bad news for you."

My adrenalin was pumping. Could this be my big break? I wondered. But then what could the bad news be?

"The good news," he said, "is we want to make you an associate producer."

Wow! A golden opportunity, I thought.

"The bad news," he continued with a grin, "is that you'll be working the early morning shift, which begins at 2 A.M."

I smiled halfheartedly, accepted the offer—though I felt exhausted just pondering what working those hours would be like—and embarked on what would turn out to be a short but valuable experience.

I needed to be at work by 2:00 A.M. because we had to be on the air with our first program at 4:00 A.M., or 7:00 A.M. eastern time. The job meant going to bed at around 5:00 P.M. so I could get up shortly after midnight, shower, try to stomach a little food, and make the half-hour drive to work. (This was really no drive at all for L.A. standards. Half past one in the morning is about the only time you don't have to fight bumper-to-bumper traffic on the freeways).

I was still single at the time, and needless to say, the job meant giving up any semblance of a social life during the week—another of the sacrifices one makes while paying the dues in this business!

The work itself, however, was enjoyable. I had the run of the station when I arrived hours before the crack of dawn—no one else there but a security guard. I picked out sound bites from interviews taped the previous day and set aside important financial and political news pulled from an abundance of wire copy.

When early-morning anchor Arthur Alpert arrived, he and I used the information from the wire copy to write the first live news updates of the day. And drawing on a few decades of experience under his belt, Alpert offered me a piece of valuable advice on broadcast writing. "Write for the ear, my friend, not the eye," he said. Arthur, wherever you are, I'm still working on it.

Later in the morning, during our first full hour of live news broadcasting from L.A. and New York, I joined the show's producer and director in the booth, the station's command center. My job was to maintain contact via phone with a similar control room in New York to make sure we got in and out of each segment on time. That's when I got my first taste of the enormous pressure that comes with trying to make a live program run smoothly.

It's incredibly exhilarating when a live show goes well. There's nothing quite like it. But every once in a while the experience can be terribly frustrating. Storms can knock out satellite transmissions. Or people can simply make mistakes. When such things happen, working in the booth can be an ear-opening experience. I thought I'd heard, and used, every foul word in the book. But when tension peaked, as it often does in the booth, angry directors and producers let loose language strong enough to make even the most crass cringe.

That, however, isn't why I left FNN. After the better part of a year there, I found myself in somewhat of a Catch-22. I had decided to go back to school for a master's degree in journalism. Although I was picking up valuable TV news experience, I wasn't making enough money to put any aside for graduate school. So I resumed teaching tennis at a club in Los Angeles, where I doubled my earnings and had time for some free-lance writing. I even spent a couple of months in the Philippines helping the Associated Press (AP) cover the demonstrations and other political turmoil leading to the overthrow of the Marcos regime.

The hands-on experience at AP and FNN undoubtedly helped me get into the highly practical master's program at Northwestern University's Medill School of Journalism and paid off later in my various job searches.

Field Producers

The largest stations and networks, including cable news and sports organizations, employ some *field, special projects,* or *segment producers.* Like reporters, field producers spend a great deal of time away from the station, gathering information, conducting interviews, and working with photographers to get the right shots and natural sound needed to present a particular story.

Well-established field producers write and supervise the videotape editing of their own stories. Others less experienced merely help reporters gather the necessary elements. Regardless of who writes the story, any voice work is almost always left to a reporter or anchor. Field producers are seldom called upon to narrate.

The advantage is that it's generally easier to work one's way into a field producer job with a major news organization than it is to land a reporter position there. The field producer need not be as concerned with on-camera appearance and voice quality, though his or her newsgathering and writing skills need to be every bit as strong as those of a reporter.

Many of the top-quality, in-depth segments we see on such network newsmagazine shows as ABC's "20/20," CBS's "48 Hours," and "Dateline NBC" are put together by segment producers with many years of experience in the field.

Assignment Editors

Assignment editors at many small and medium stations rank second in the hierarchy of newsroom management, reporting to the news director. In larger markets, however, they may answer to managing editors, executive producers, or assistant news directors. But regardless of where they work, assignment editors must develop a sensitive nose for news. They work with producers in selecting which stories the station will cover on a given day—those stories they believe to be most important or interesting to their viewers.

The efforts of assignment editors can perhaps best be seen on the large assignment board they maintain—usually hung on the newsroom wall in a highly visible spot. They keep that board updated throughout the day with the catchy slugs (titles) of each story being covered, the names of the reporters, photographers, or other crew members assigned to those stories, the extent of coverage the stories warrant, the shooting times and locations, and the particular newscast for which each story is slated. Assignment editors at the networks and many local stations keep that same information updated on computers as well.

Although the extent of their responsibilities varies greatly from station to station, assignment editors invariably assure the right stories get the coverage they warrant by planning the efforts of field crews and making sure those plans are carried out.

"It's tough to coordinate the coverage of stories," says Tom Anthony, a former TV news director in the Northeast who runs the assignment desk at CNBC. "You've got to be creative, focusing on the most important stories and sometimes putting the least important stories on the back burner."

KNOWING YOUR GEOGRAPHY

A strong working knowledge of the lay of the land and a collection of city and regional maps are essential. The assignment editor must be able to quickly figure out which news crew in the field is closest to a breaking story, and then communicate to that crew via two-way radio or telephone the fastest route for getting there. Road, traffic, and weather conditions must be taken into account when making such decisions.

"Assignment editors need a real talent for problem-solving," says Anthony. "If you have that talent, you'll help the news organization move ahead and you'll go far."

Assignment editors must be aggressive, yet patient, prepared each day to deal with a certain amount of rejection. They spend a great deal of time on the phone trying to set up interviews, often making dozens of calls before finally convincing someone to talk on-camera about a sensitive issue.

"You also end up relying on the graciousness of interview subjects to accommodate you at the moment you need them," Anthony says. "The very nature of this business means that we just can't work our schedules around the schedules of the people we need to talk to, given our deadlines."

Sometimes the search for a "soundbite" bears no fruit. Other times, it results in a highly rewarding, exclusive interview.

THE VIRTUE OF PATIENCE

Assignment editors must also be tactful, to avoid upsetting a temperamental reporter or photographer to whom they must assign the day's more boring story or an event that may never materialize. I've often been assigned to cover city council meetings where the most inflammatory issues on the agenda sparked no debate at all and the highlight of the evening was a decision to grant a special liquor permit to the local Elks Club for a fundraiser—not exactly a lead story, or any story for that matter. Nevertheless, it was important to be there just in case.

"Sometimes you have to take chances," says Anthony. "You have to really sell a story because the merits may be hidden. But together with reporters we can focus on what's really important about a story and get a great one on the air."

Tact and patience also come in handy for the assignment editor when explaining to impatient members of the community, in the kindest tone of voice, why the station wasn't able to cover a particular story important to them. The following is much like many conversations I've heard coming from the assignment desk:

"I'm so sorry we weren't able to get anyone to your grandmother's 100th birthday party, Mrs. Jones. Our crews had to cover the big fire that broke out downtown and the Mayor's announcement that he's going to step down from office. But we sure hope it was a great birthday party, and we promise to try again next year."

Anthony says dealing with such issues isn't nearly as frustrating as actually shooting a story, then failing to get the piece on the air.

"Sometimes you shoot it, with a reporter on the scene, and you go the whole nine yards and someone, usually a producer, knocks it out of the show," he says. "That's when it's really tough to explain to somebody that we tried, but we just couldn't make it on the air."

COMMUNITY AWARENESS

The assignment editor has to be aware of just about everything going on in the community, relying heavily on press releases, wirecopy, newspapers, and a strong network of personal contacts to provide the locations and times of scheduled events. It's also imperative to use those sources to build background files on the various issues affecting the community. That information may be needed at any time as stories unfold, or on slow news days when assignment editors must come up with innovative story ideas.

"We're a central clearinghouse for the farming out of ideas," Anthony says. "It's a challenge to come up with enough interesting and compelling stories each day for the troops to work on. Constant reading, constant listening, constant questioning of the people out there who are your best news sources, and regular input from the reporters provide good story ideas. You're constantly being graded on that basis."

One of those who's done such grading as a news director and senior producer is Jamie Avery.

"There's never a slow news day—just slow desk people and reporters not generating enough ideas," he says. "There are always interesting things out there to cover."

As for breaking news, assignment editors at local stations must keep an ear attuned to the scanner, which monitors the activities of law enforcement agencies and fire departments. And as a safeguard, regular "beat checks" must be made—that is, calling the police and fire departments every few hours to make sure no newsworthy incident has gone unnoticed. Beat checks may also include hospitals, government offices, courts, and any other valuable contacts.

REWARDS WITHOUT GLORY

Working as an assignment editor is a constantly challenging, yet seemingly thankless, job which offers little more glory than the credit occasionally shown on the screen at the end of a newscast.

"It's the highly visible on-air people who get most of the recognition," says Anthony. "Very little praise gets heaped upon assignment editors.

The rewards are hard to pin down. It's just the way you feel about it yourself. The job is especially rewarding when the next day you see a story in the newspaper that you got on the air the day before, especially because we're accused so often of taking newspaper stories and just adapting them for television."

While providing a rewarding challenge for those strong at heart, the job of assignment editor also serves as a stepping stone to higher news management.

"How far assignment editors go in the business depends on their news judgment, how well spoken they are, and how well they're able to play newsroom politics," says Avery, a former news director in Harrisburg, Pennsylvania. "It's not just how well they do their job. A lot depends on who they align themselves with."

Assignment editors often become managing editors, assistant news directors, and news directors, steering the entire news department and overseeing the production of its shows.

News Directors

The news director heads all news operations at the station, including weather and sports. He or she has the final say on what stories will be reported and the type of coverage they warrant. The solid news judgment exhibited by most successful news directors is the result of the insight they gained during years of working their way up the newsroom ladder.

News directors play two roles: journalist and manager. In some small markets, they even anchor, report, and produce the news. But in all markets, they are the team leaders responsible for the ratings of their news programs. They do the hiring and firing in the news department, trying to assemble the strongest team possible.

THE BOSS AND THE BOTTOM LINE

News directors who achieve high ratings are eagerly recruited by larger stations. High ratings draw more advertisers to a station and allow the sales department to charge them larger fees for the airing of commercials. That, in turn, can protect a news department's budget and the jobs of newsroom employees. It's the constant, sometimes desperate, effort to draw a greater audience that causes some news directors to focus their staffs' attention on more popular, sensational or risqué issues during certain times of the year known as ratings periods, or "sweeps."

"You certainly are more involved in marketing the product and taking care of promotions during ratings periods," says Terry Baker, a senior producer at CNBC and former news director at WNBC-TV in New York. "You become much more of a marketer—certainly more than we prefer."

Keep in mind that ratings, often boosted by bikini-clad women on beaches, don't necessarily reflect the quality of newscasts, at least from this journalist's perspective.

News directors are also responsible for the news department's budget, and answerable to the station's general manager. In this day and age of fiscal restraint, that can be an unenviable, tough spot to be in. News directors often find themselves sandwiched between a station's upper management, trying to limit spending to protect the "bottom line," and the news staff, lobbying for more spending on equipment and salaries. It's not the easiest way to make friends.

"You're trying to juggle the competing aspects of being a journalist—doing what's right newswise, and being a manager," says Baker. "It's a job that can be very pressure-packed, especially if you have a boss who doesn't understand all that."

"A lot of television stations, as is true with a lot of businesses now, are overleveraged," says Eskridge. "They took on too much debt in the 1980s. That, combined with more competition now from cable and independent stations, means they're even under greater financial pressure than they normally would be. Since the news operation of a station is often the biggest part, or ought to be the biggest part, of their operating budget, that department feels the pinch most."

THE REVOLVING DOOR

News directors do indeed have a lot riding on their ability to boost ratings on a tight budget. When ratings drop, they, like anchors, are often the first to be told to pack their bags. The turnover rate for news directors is very high.

"It's sort of like getting rid of the manager of a baseball team," said Eskridge. "You can't fire the whole team when things are going bad."

Vernon Stone, Professor of Journalism at the University of Missouri, Columbia, and Director of Research for the Radio-Television News Directors Association, has closely studied the turnover rate among newsroom leaders across the country. His nationwide surveys show that in recent years TV news directors have held their jobs for an average of two to three years before being fired or moving on to greener pastures. Only about five percent of them have been at the same station for 11 years or more.

"The managerial revolving door is still the rule in many newsrooms," Stone says.

Yet many news managers are willing to take on that risk in exchange for the excitement of leading a team into the daily challenge of covering the most important events.

NOTE OF DISTINCTION

News directors are not to be confused with directors and technical directors, who from the booth command the studio camera operators and call the shots during a live broadcast. Directors usually work their way up on a station's technical, not newsgathering, staff. They're in charge of steering the ship through choppy waters on the way to fulfilling the technical end of the producer's journalistic game plan.

ENG Photographers, Videotape Editors, and Sound Technicians

SHOOTING FOR SUCCESS

If you have a good eye for composition, a steady hand, and a strong back for carrying around heavy camera equipment, often on the run, you may find your niche on the frontlines as an ENG (electronic news gathering) photographer, also known in the business as a "photog," or "shooter."

Photographers must often muscle their way into the midst of breaking stories, though the level of action varies greatly from day to day. One day a photographer may cover a fire, a fatal car accident, a shooting, a sports event, or all four stories in one day. And then the next day's most thrilling event might be a meeting of the city's planning and zoning commission, where minutes often seem like hours.

But no matter how little the action, it's the job of the photographer to capture the shots needed by the videotape editor to make each story look good.

"The first editing that takes place is in the field with a camera," says veteran videotape editor Bart Cannistra of KNBC-TV in Los Angeles. "The first edit occurs when you turn on the camera, shoot your first shot and ask your first question.

"From an editor's perspective, unless you have good shots to work with in the editing room, you're locked into doing the story in one way," says Cannistra. "You need options, so you can choose the better approach and make the most of the video."

MORE THAN JUST PICTURES

Some photographers prefer the title "photojournalist," an accurate billing, especially in small markets, because they often wear the hats of both photographer *and* journalist. When reporters aren't available to accompany photographers in the field, or when shooters working solo happen upon breaking stories, they must ask the questions and gather details much as a reporter would.

"Especially in small markets, where most of us start, you get a lot of stories that you have to cover yourself," says John Mason, a photographer at KTVK-TV in Phoenix who started out in the business in Colorado Springs. "Sometimes you shoot whole packages by yourself, rushing from one place to another with all the equipment, and jotting down information. But that experience is the key. You're certainly not in it for the money, at least not in the beginning."

TRAINING THE EYE

Technical training in school or during internships helps some people land jobs right away as field photographers at small stations. Most of them are already proficient at setting up appropriate lighting equipment, operating the camera, and recording natural sound. Others get started in the business operating studio cameras, with guidance from the director during newscasts on how to frame the shots.

Some photographers in large markets start out as audio technicians, gathering natural sound while working side by side with, and closely watching, experienced field photographers. A few others begin as videotape editors, learning how stories are shot as they piece together the footage shooters bring back to the station.

SHARP EDITING

Some photographers become videotape editors, though neither shooting nor editing is a prerequisite for the other. Good editors can work their way into successful careers in large markets, expertly combining the best shots and sound captured by photographers and audio technicians into compelling packages.

"It's our job to try to make even mundane stories move at a good pace— getting to the main points early and making it look clean," says Cannistra. "The stories can't be cluttered with a bunch of vague images and boring narration.

"We try to cover stories with interesting video that's applicable," he continues. "That means going outside the boring city council chamber to illustrate the issues or problems that have prompted the action or legislation. If a bunch of accidents have occurred at traffic lights, for example, and the city council is discussing ways to avoid that, we'd want to show shots of those intersections and maybe even accidents that have happened there.

"The biggest challenge in editing is to tell the story well in a short amount of time and with the materials provided," Cannistra adds. "When I can do that, I feel good about my work. It's also nice sometimes to be able to take more time on features—stories providing more substance."

COMPLEMENTARY SKILLS

In most small and many medium markets, photographers, reporters, and producers edit much of their own material. The number of videotape editor positions at those stations is often limited to one or two. Some small stations don't have any editor slots. So, unlike most photographers who have no choice but to start out in small markets, quite a few successful videotape editors get their technical training in bigger shops.

Regardless of where they're working, photographers and editors learn and improve from hands-on experience, and often by trial and error. Both use their own judgment and taste. Yet they need also to communicate well with each other and the writer to maximize the impact of the package.

"When I do work with a reporter, consulting with him on what we're going to do and maybe doing it a little differently than the other guys is really important," says Mason. "We try to be somewhat creative. Instead of just doing the basic sit-down interview, for example, we might put a wireless microphone on the interviewee. Then we can talk to him while following him around as he does what he normally does."

SOUNDING GOOD

Just as stations have phased out some engineering jobs with the use of more efficient equipment, many no longer include sound technicians in their field crews. Many of the new videotape cameras have the audio controls built in, making it easier for a photographer to regulate sound as well as the shot, and in the eyes of budget-conscious stations eliminating the need for a separate soundperson.

Still, some major news organizations employ audio specialists in the field when the gathering of just the right amount of natural sound is of the utmost importance. Sound technicians are adept at operating special extended microphones and other audio recording equipment.

Sports Anchors and Reporters

Remember the boy or girl who back in grade school could cite the batting average of just about any professional baseball player and the number of yards gained each game by the NFL's leading rushers? That kind of love for sports and mind for detail are what it takes to become a successful sports anchor, reporter or producer, along with an ability to communicate the information in an entertaining manner.

Sportscasters generally have greater "creative license" in terms of writing and on-air delivery than those of us in news. But much of what was written in the previous "News Reporters" and "News Anchors" sections about the racing around town, crazy schedules, and tight deadlines applies to covering sports as well.

LITTLE LEAGUES AND BEYOND

Like their counterparts in news, aspiring sports reporters and anchors must be willing to spend a few years in small and medium markets, focusing as much, if not more, on local high school and college games as on the national sports scene. Some get lucky and find their first jobs not far from larger cities where they can occasionally cover first-hand a professional team or two.

"The scope of things you have to cover is enormous," says Mark Olesh, a talented sports anchor in his second television job at KERO-TV in Bakersfield, California. "You've got the nearby big-city stuff [in Los Angeles] and all the high school and other local events to cover. So reading as much material as you can becomes the key. It's a real must—getting to know all the details and background.

CBS Sportscaster Greg Gumbel agrees, adding that the reading load only grows larger as one's career in sports reporting blossoms and the scope of coverage increases.

"I probably do two to three hours of reading each day," says Gumble. "I read every newspaper and magazine I can get my hands on. And when I'm preparing for something like the NCAA [basketball] tournament, I spend up to five or six hours a day reading background material."

Although big and small-market sportscasters have a great deal of reading in common, the ways in which they cover sports differ.

"Since we're not covering as many professional teams, our whole approach to sports has to be different—a little softer," Olesh says. "Unlike the guys at the networks, who can be very critical of professional athletes, we can't just attack or jump all over amateur athletes who make big mistakes."

Indeed, communities are far more forgiving of their own amateur athletes who've yet to enter the high-paying professional sports arena.

At many small and medium stations, the sports staff consists of just two people. One of them anchors the sports during the week, the other does so on weekends. Both are responsible for the necessary field reporting, and often must shoot the events themselves for lack of a spare photographer. It's also their job to generate plenty of fresh story ideas and produce colorful sidebars to ongoing stories.

The hours are long and erratic, given the numerous sporting events at night and on weekends. For that reason, a genuine love for sports is imperative. Besides, viewers can usually tell by the level of enthusiasm whether sports reporters and anchors truly enjoy what they're doing.

All that enjoyable, hard work pays off in greater dividends for sports reporters and anchors who make it to big markets. Although their hours remain long and varied, they get more help from researchers, producers, and photographers. That assistance frees them up to do more of what they love most—writing and enthusiastically delivering the latest in sports information.

Sports Producers

Small stations generally don't employ sports producers per se, relying instead on the sports reporters and anchors to produce all their own material. Therefore, some aspiring sports producers start out as production assistants or in other entry-level jobs in big markets—at local stations, cable channels, or the networks. There, they begin to get the writing and technical production experience necessary to put together exciting sports stories. That's great for those who know right away that they want to write and produce.

But for those who aren't sure whether they want to work behind the scenes or on-camera in sports, small markets provide the opportunity to do it all, and then move in the direction of greatest interest. Some small-market sports reporters and anchors use the wide range of experience they've gained to land jobs as sports producers in larger markets.

Weather Reporters/Meteorologists

PERSONALITY FIRST

Some well-known television personalities have effectively used weather reporting jobs to help launch their careers in show business, relying heavily on wirecopy for the weather information they needed. David Letterman started out in television as a weatherman. So did Pat Sajak, of *Wheel of Fortune* fame. Neither was formally trained as a meteorologist.

There are still opportunities to break into TV weather forecasting, usually in small and medium markets, without substantial knowledge about the science of meteorology. Some stations look first and foremost for outgoing personalities willing to learn about weather on the job. After all, the wire services and computer technology available today explain just about everything one needs to know. And a good on-camera communicator can make it appear that he is indeed an expert meteorologist, or at least make the audience forget that he's not.

"After a couple of job searches, I came up with the theory that if weather experts were all they [news directors] wanted, they'd just go grab someone out of weather training centers and the National Weather Service," says Len Johnson, a weathercaster at Fox Television's WBFF-TV in Baltimore. "They're looking for more than that. It must be personality first. The weather basics can be learned pretty quickly.

"No one cares how high the clouds are," continues Johnson, who after landing his first weathercasting job in Reno, Nevada, took a few college meteorology courses. "Believe me, no one cares about cloud-deck heights, jet streams, and radar loops. You can't get caught up too much in details and forget to tell people whether it'll rain or snow the next day. That's what's important to them—generalities instead of details.

"Some education about weather can help a news director sell you to his station's general manager, so he can cover his tail with management as far as credibility goes," Johnson adds. "But the most important thing is they want someone in who will draw numbers (more viewers and good ratings)."

Other stations, however, especially in regions plagued by tumultuous weather, require weather reporters to demonstrate a thorough knowledge of, and legitimate interest in, meteorology and the latest computerized weather-predicting technology. That may mean having a meteorology or related degree and/or national certification. Many stations in agricultural areas, for example, where farmers depend on detailed weather information, look for the on-air insight of legitimate meteorologists.

Expertise in meteorology *and* a colorful personality can't be beat in the TV weather forecasting business. That combination makes for fun-to-watch, credible weather segments, not to mention the wonders it can do for a station's ratings.

■3■
Matching Education with Jobs

In today's highly competitive job market most news directors strongly recommend, and many require, a college degree for just about any job in television news. Exceptions are occasionally made, however, for those on the technical side or those who may be switching careers and have other valuable work experience.

Opinions vary greatly on which degrees are good for which jobs. And the degree itself may not be as important as the classes taken, or the internships held. Since news directors usually do the hiring in TV news, it's helpful to understand how they see things.

Polishing the Prose

Vernon Stone, a University of Missouri journalism professor who serves as research director for the Radio-Television News Directors Association (RTNDA), recently conducted a national survey of 434 TV news directors. More than half said the college courses that had helped them most in their careers were writing, journalism, and broadcasting. Other popular courses with news directors were history, political science, and other social studies.

"The finding reconfirms that writing is at the heart of broadcast journal-

30

ism and should be central to education for careers in radio and TV news," Stone wrote.

"Good writing and the clear thinking that relates to clear writing develop from a long process of individual practice and critique. News directors say writing courses are the ones that have helped them most, and they expect the newspeople they hire to bring writing ability to the job. On the job, news directors and other supervisors can help writers add professional polish. But the basics need to be learned in school."

A study by Frank N. Magid Associates for the RTNDA reached a similar conclusion. It found that for those in search of on-camera jobs, the abilities to think, write, and speak clearly are paramount in the eyes of news directors.

Broadening the Background

More than 75 percent of the news directors responding to Stone's survey had earned college degrees. Only 3 percent had never gone to college. More than 60 percent of those who were college trained had majored in journalism, radio-TV, mass media, and other communications studies, as opposed to only 40 percent two decades ago. Fourteen percent reported having majored in social studies. English majors made up 8 percent.

At least 25 percent of the news directors said they'd take more social studies if they had it to do all over again. Subjects such as history, political science, and sociology combine research and writing skills and offer insight into the modern trends and theories relating to topics often covered by news teams.

Ann Compton says a liberal arts background is imperative. "I'm not a fan of undergraduate journalism schools," she states emphatically, saying students are better off getting a "broader" education, and learning to be broadcast journalists on the job.

"If I were doing the hiring," adds Compton, "I'd prefer to see a liberal arts or social studies background with courses of substance such as history, economics, and literature."

The Practical Approach

There's no doubt, however, that at least some broadcast news experience, whether gained in school or during an internship, is needed before seeking that first job in the business. It's not impossible to find entry-level jobs without any broadcasting experience, but news directors definitely favor applicants who have already mastered some of the basic skills required in the newsroom.

And for those of you aspiring to one day manage a newsroom, it might be interesting to note another of Vernon Stone's findings—that most news directors wish they'd taken more business courses in college because they spend more time on managerial than on journalistic activities.

What's in a Name?

Regardless of which courses you take, most news directors this reporter has talked to say the quality and diversity of those classes, combined with some hands-on broadcasting experience, are far more important than where you studied.

Make no mistake, however. Attending a school with a fine reputation certainly can't hurt and may in fact open a few more doors. Many of the top-notch colleges and trade schools have set up alumni networks to help graduates find their first jobs in broadcast journalism.

How Helpful are Graduate Degrees? (Isn't Undergraduate Work Enough?)

Some new directors are impressed by graduate degrees in journalism, liberal arts, or specialized fields of study that may lend expertise to news reporting. Other news directors couldn't care less. But again, they're all impressed with hands-on experience in broadcasting.

A master's degree in journalism is therefore most valuable if obtained at a school offering practical broadcasting experience or access to internships at nearby stations.

Rick Brown offers the following advice: "Journalists need to be well-rounded. So a good way to go is to get a good liberal arts education as an undergraduate, then go to the good nuts and bolts—a short, practical graduate program that gives you everyday reporting experience."

As for those students who have already gained daily reporting experience in an undergraduate broadcast journalism program, Brown and other news managers see little need to repeat those efforts at the graduate level.

Worthwhile Investment

More graduate programs than ever are offering the kind of full-time, daily reporting opportunities one gets at that first job in the business. Such schools can be expensive. But an investment in the right program can go a long way toward fully preparing the student for the real world of broadcast news. Among other things, a strong graduate program affords one the opportunity to put together high-quality audition, or *resume*, tapes—videotape samples of one's work. Those tapes, in turn, can be very influential in landing a job in television news, whether in reporting, anchoring, producing, photographing, or editing.

It should be noted that plenty of undergraduate and trade school broadcast journalism programs also provide practical experience and the chance to build strong audition tapes.

Setting an Example

The undergraduate and graduate broadcast journalism programs at Northwestern University and the University of Missouri are among the best. At Northwestern's Medill School of Journalism, a unique one-year master's program develops and fine-tunes broadcast journalism skills.

During the first six months the curriculum's emphasis is actually on print journalism—great training for anyone. Then the students most interested in broadcast news break away and spend the second half of the year producing and reporting television and radio stories out of newsrooms in Chicago and Washington, DC. Talk about hands-on training!

Learning to Localize

In Washington the students cover and localize stories for TV and radio stations around the country that subscribe to The Medill News Service.

Localizing a story means focusing on how a national or international issue affects the viewers to whom you're broadcasting in a particular part of the country.

While in the graduate program at Medill and working as the Washington correspondent for WIBW-TV and Radio in Topeka, Kansas, I learned that a new type of telecommunications device for the deaf was being hooked up to phones on Capitol Hill. I asked around and found that one had been installed in Senator Bob Dole's Washington office. The local angle in the story was obvious: the hearing-impaired in Kansas could communicate their concerns to Dole's Washington staff, and the senator, thinking about a run for the presidency at the time, could score points with his constituents.

But it's not always easy to localize stories. Some attempts don't work out. When I covered a protest on the steps of the Capitol against U.S. aid to the guerrillas fighting Nicaragua's Sandinista government, I had been told a group from Topeka and other parts of Kansas would participate. A photographer and I searched long and hard, asking demonstrators where they were from; we felt a bit like Dorothy in *The Wizard of Oz*— looking for Kansas. Unfortunately, ours wasn't just a bad dream, and we never did find anyone from "home."

I packaged the story on the protest anyway and sent it to WIBW-TV. But without any comments from Kansans or even shots of them taking part in the demonstration, I can't blame the station for not airing the piece. Nothing in it pertained specifically to Kansas, let alone Topeka.

Winning Combination

The combination of a master's degree and on-the-job experience can be especially valuable for those who want to teach journalism at the college level. If teaching isn't in your career plan, many news directors and other seasoned veterans will tell you to forget grad school. They'll tell you the first job beats sitting in a classroom and theorizing about journalism any day. But they fail to take into account the graduate programs supervised by experienced professionals where students spend a great deal of time getting hands-on experience *and* an abundance of constructive criticism. Such feedback is hard to come by in TV newsrooms, where the news director is swamped with many other tasks at hand.

Enjoyable readings and seminars provide graduate students with knowledge about the important legal and ethical framework within which journalists operate, as well as the history and development of the trade. In addition, journalism schools are ideal places to begin developing a network of contacts that could pay off for years to come.

"The sorority or fraternity of journalists is greatly important in this business," says Lou Prato, who heads Northwestern's Medill News Service in Washington, DC, and is treasurer of the Radio-Television News Directors Association. "My personal belief is that a graduate degree helps you no matter what you do twenty years from now."

It is largely a personal choice. I opted to get a master's degree in journalism because I've always placed a good deal of emphasis on my own education. I'm one of those people who thinks you can never get enough of it. I truly believe the education has enriched me and added to my credibility and success as a broadcast journalist.

Finding the Right School

More than 300 schools in the United States offer substantial two-year, four-year, and graduate television and radio programs. Take a close look at the programs to see which one suits you best. State, or public, universities offer some of the finest broadcast journalism programs, usually at little cost to state residents. And while the cost of attending a private college may seem prohibitive, many of those schools offer helpful financial aid and scholarship programs.

For information on those schools, contact

President, Broadcast Education Association
National Association of Broadcasters
1771 N Street, N.W.
Washington, DC 20036
(202) 429-5355

The Radio and Television News Directors Foundation, a division of the Radio-Television News Directors Association, offers scholarships for undergraduate and graduate broadcast journalism students. For information contact

RTNDA
1717 K Street, N.W.
Washington, DC 20006
(202) 659-6510

Alpha Epsilon Rho of the National Broadcasting Society has chapters at more than 100 colleges and universities in the United States. During the school year the group publishes a monthly newsletter for student and professional members. It also conducts informative annual and regional conventions and workshops designed to bridge the gap between students and the professional broadcasting world. For more information, write to

National Executive Secretary
National Broadcasting Society, AERho
College of Journalism
University of South Carolina
Columbia, SC 29208

If you can't, or don't want to, spend the time and money on a graduate program, start pounding the pavement. *Persistence* is just as important as any degree in landing that first job in the business and moving up the newsroom ladder.

■ 4 ■

Internships and Other News Media Experience

Earning Nothing but Experience

Beggars can't be choosers. If you don't have any experience in television news, you've got to be willing to take about any job in the business to get a foot in the door. That includes nonpaying internships, plenty of which can be found at local stations, networks, and the fast-growing number of cable operations. You may have to work at another station while interning. But that's all part of paying the dues.

Even a part-time internship is likely to provide you with a golden opportunity to learn a great deal about TV news. Eventually, it may also give you the chance to put together an audition tape in your spare time with the help of the station's staff and equipment. The samples of your work on that tape will help you find a full-time job in the business at that station or elsewhere.

Internships are a great way to meet experienced newspeople with whom you'll want to stay in touch for help in the future. The name of the game is *networking*, also referred to as schmoozing. Some consider this means being fawning and ingratiating, but you need only to be sincere. Put your

37

nose to the grindstone and prove to them you want to succeed in a business you truly care about.

Never Too Early, Never Too Late

Try to intern as soon as you decide you want a career in television news, or even if you just think it's a possibility. That means as early as high school in some cases, college in others, and even much later for those switching careers.

At the age of 44, and with the youngest of his four children already in high school, Ken Moon left behind a successful home-building business in the Colorado Springs–Pueblo area to pursue his longtime dream—a job as a TV news reporter.

"When you get to be in your mid-40s, you begin to realize the end is closer than the beginning," Moon says. "So, if you're going to ever do it, you do it. And I decided I had to try it. I didn't want to say, 'I never gave it a shot.' "

After taking some broadcasting courses at a nearby college, Moon interned at KRDO-TV in Colorado Springs. He gives the following account of how he got the internship:

"I showed up at Channel 13 and said, 'I want to do anything you guys want me to do. I'll show up on time and I'll work for free, at least for now. I'm very reliable and you'll like what I do.' "

Within months Moon parlayed that positive, willing-to-work attitude into a full-time reporter job.

"I think that volunteering is where it's at, instead of wanting to start at the top or in the middle," he says. "You give them something they need, which is free labor or covering an odd shift or weird hours, and you get your foot in the door. And the business is so changeable that five minutes after you walk in somebody quits and leaves, and you move up."

While still in college in West Virginia, Terry Baker interned at a small nearby TV station, where he was allowed to produce, write, report, and even anchor the news. That experience helped him land another internship after college in Baltimore.

"I came out of college with some very practical, hands-on experience," Baker says. "I knew how to write. I could put together a TV news program. And I had made very important professional contacts. That all helped me get my first professional job at the Baltimore station—first as a desk assistant, then eventually as a producer. The bottom line is that I ultimately got the job where I interned."

Baker later took his producing skills to New York's WNBC-TV, where he capped a ten-year stay with two years as news director before moving on to CNBC's "The Real Story" as a senior producer.

Moving from Radio to TV

Working at radio stations can provide writing and voice experience helpful in landing a TV news job. The rigid deadlines are similar, as is the necessary broadcast writing style: concise and conversational. And like their counterparts in television, radio reporters spend a good deal of time covering breaking news (news as it happens on the spot).

"Radio training doesn't hinder you in any way for television," says Cokie Roberts, who has spent many years working as a news correspondent in both TV and radio. "In radio you learn how to tell a story quickly, cogently, and in a clear fashion. That works for any medium."

Roberts says writers just starting out in broadcasting, whether in television or radio, must learn to keep their stories simple.

"Beginners tend to report too long. They tell you everything they know because they simply don't have the confidence to sort out all the information and tell a straightforward story."

But there are vast differences as well between radio and TV news. The radio writer must draw pictures with words. The TV writer uses words to complement pictures, letting some of the video and sound speak for themselves.

"That's the main difference in writing for TV—that you're writing to pictures," says Roberts. "The pictures are so important that you even have to leave things out occasionally when you don't have pictures to go along with them."

Another significant difference between the two media is that radio writers, especially those at commercial stations (as opposed to public, or noncommercial, stations), are often under even tighter time constraints and deadlines than their counterparts in television.

"When you write for commercial radio, you're writing short, all-inclusive spots with the main points only," says Roberts.

The differences between radio and TV newswriting, however, pale in comparison to the valuable preparation radio newswriting provides for would-be TV newswriters and reporters.

For those of you interested in sports, radio stations are good places to get your feet wet in play-by-play and other forms of sports reporting and producing. But as on the news side, radio sportswriting differs from that of television. Again, the radio writer must draw clear pictures with words. TV sports reporters and producers must write very closely to the pictures and natural sound available.

Nothing Beats TV

Although many radio writers and broadcasters have successfully made the transition into television, most people in the broadcasting business agree there's no better training ground for TV news than the TV newsroom. So if that's the direction in which you're headed, keep your eyes on the prize.

"A tremendous number of people have come from radio to television news—not just the 'old guard,' " says Roberts. "Radio is still a good way in. But in general, the best way to get into television is by doing television."

The Transition from Print

It's true that nothing substitutes for hands-on TV news experience. But newspapers and magazines, like radio, can provide future TV journalists with valuable experience.

Researching and writing for the so-called print media provide a solid foundation for thorough, accurate reporting. Print and broadcast writing styles, however, remain far apart. Although some publications, such as Gannett's *USA Today*, employ a TV newslike technique of succinctly bringing out just the main points or highlights of stories, many others still pack long sentences full of detail. They offer the reader a great deal of background and plenty of perspective, but in ways unsuitable for TV news.

Newspaper and magazine readers can mull over a paragraph, time and time again, at their own pace. But TV viewers only have one chance to see and hear a story (assuming they don't record it on videotape) before it passes into what I call airwave infinity. That means sentences must be kept short and simple—some prefer to describe the style as conversational. And they must be written to complement the video.

Making the transition from print to broadcast writing is difficult enough. But there are other differences, too. Print journalists in the field need only a pen, a notepad, and sometimes a small audiocassette recorder. Television journalists must tote around quite a bit of heavy machinery, since they rely on cameras, sound-gathering equipment, and lights to capture the essence of stories. All that equipment means a greater likelihood of technical problems, and thus occasional difficulties in gathering the various elements of a story.

"Teamwork becomes much more important in television," says Pam Zekman, who started her career in the newspaper business. "Focusing on the performance end, and learning to feel comfortable with that, was a big change. And getting the pictures can be tough. The targets of investigations don't exactly pose for the cameras.

"But it is a lot of fun. TV reporting is challenging, and when it's well-done and works, it's great, and really adds to the story. The impact is so much greater than in print, and it's very rewarding."

Finding or Creating a Prosperous Internship

If you're a student, talk to a school counselor about the courses, part-time jobs, and internships in broadcasting that might be available on campus or at professional TV or radio stations in the community. If that doesn't work, approach the stations directly. If they don't already offer internship programs, explain why they should. Tell them they'll gain from your labor without having to pay you anything. You'll gain from the experience.

Get your hands on everything you can during an internship to learn as much as possible about every aspect of the broadcast news business. Offer to do everything and anything.

"We provide the opportunity for interns to make tapes of themselves anchoring in the studio or reporting out in the field," says KNBC-TV's Bart Cannistra. "And we'll show them how to use the cameras and other equipment. The stuff they do doesn't make the air, but it's only intended to give them experience and help them get a job out there. I would tell any intern to really take advantage of the opportunity and the good graces of the people that work at the station."

Every bit of experience you pick up in an internship will weigh in your favor. It could make the difference between you and the hundreds of others applying for jobs at the same station.

Vacation Opportunities

In the largest markets vacation-relief jobs, usually during summers and holiday seasons, allow a few of those who want to work behind the scenes to get a foot in the door, often as production or newsdesk assistants. That may mean taking on such unchallenging tasks as "ripping" scripts and wire copy, or "running" tapes back to the station from crews in the field.

Vacation-relief positions are only temporary. When the vacation ends, so does the job, with no guarantee of work in the future. But the experience affords one the golden opportunity to meet, impress, and stay in contact with people who could be helpful in landing a permanent job in the future.

■ 5 ■

Where to Start: The Boonies versus the Big Leagues

Many of today's top TV news veterans got their first jobs in the business in big markets. In those days there were fewer TV stations, most of them located in the largest cities. There are now many more broadcast and cable TV news operations. But the popularity of electronic journalism has made it imperative that most people just starting out in the business do so at small-market stations, somewhere out in the "boonies," where rookies work for little more than the experience they gain. With few exceptions these days, the biggest TV news organizations hire only experienced, highly skilled newspeople.

Big Isn't Always Better

Broadcast journalists who start out in large markets run the risk of getting stuck for long periods of time, often years, in low-level jobs behind the scenes.

"It's very easy to get pigeonholed near the bottom, especially at the broadcast networks," says veteran producer Jamie Avery. "The union restrictions at the networks are such that it's hard for people just getting started to get the experience they need to move up to higher positions.

43

The smaller markets don't have the same kinds of limitations. Young producers, for example, carry a lot more responsibility in small markets and gain experience very quickly."

"You shoot, you edit, write, produce, anchor, do sports, do weather— a little bit of everything," says Marv Rockford. "If you're going to eventually end up being a producer, and you eventually want to be an executive producer or news director, a broad view of the whole playing field and all of the roles out there is not a bad foundation to have."

Jodi Fleisig couldn't agree more. She began her career as both a reporter and producer in Wausau, Wisconsin. "There's no question that starting in a small market is much better. You get to do everything. You're not just watching. You get your hands on everything, and you can expand and grow every time you move up. You learn a lot from the experience of working in different markets, at different stations, with different people."

PRODUCERS, WRITERS, AND ASSIGNMENT EDITORS

Nevertheless, some aspiring producers, writers, and assignment editors will find the long dues-paying process at the television networks and top local stations worthwhile. The inside connections they develop over the years may give them a competitive edge over outsiders when positions higher on the newsroom ladder open up. The most talented can work their way up from production assistant, or news associate (depending on the terminology used in a particular shop), to researcher, writer, or associate producer, and then finally to producer. A few continue to move up the ranks of newsroom management to executive producer, managing editor, assistant news director, . . . and news director.

When a producer or assignment editor position opens up in the newsroom, news managers must often choose between an outside candidate who has "done it all" in a smaller market and someone in-house who has shown great potential as, say, an associate producer. Many lean heavily toward promoting from within. Others strictly compare the talents of the individual candidates.

REPORTING, ANCHORING, AND SHOOTING

Those of you anxious to get into reporting, anchoring, or shooting (videography) should try to do so immediately in smaller towns. (See chapter 6 for a list of all U.S. media markets, big and small, and information on how to locate TV stations in each of the cities.)

Marv Rockford explains why very few on-air employees get their start in his town of Denver and other large markets: "You've got to be a finished product when you go on the air. News directors in this market expect you to have a fully developed set of skills when you go on the air— good news-gathering skills, good presentation skills, good production skills. You've got to have that whole package already when you come to work here for an on-air job. So you do your entry-level work in a small market."

"But it's tough for young reporters, and a lot of kids don't know about paying the dues," adds Jodi Fleisig. "If you want the glamour and prestige, forget it. You have to know you're going to have a crazy life-style . . . working holidays and weekends . . . and you've got to be willing to do the dirty work, the grunt work. In order to get strong, you've got to do lots of what might, at the time, seem like insignificant stories."

While studying communications in college, John Mason interned at Denver's highly respected ABC station, KUSA-TV. Still, it took him a year to find his first paid position as a TV news photographer in Colorado Springs, just a little more than an hour's drive south of Denver.

"After looking all over the country for a year, coast to coast, pleading for a job, I finally got a part-time job as a weekend shooter," says Mason. "I just hung in there, and after about six months it turned into a full-time job."

Three years later Mason made similar sacrifices in order to get his foot in the door of a bigger news organization. Although he had become an expert photographer, he took a job coordinating shoots on weekends and editing videotape three days during the week at ABC affiliate KTVK in Phoenix. His initial responsibilities included no shooting, the thing he loved to do most.

"So I walked into the news director's office one day, shortly after I started, and begged him to let me shoot on my days off," says Mason. "I said, 'I'll shoot whatever you need me to.' He let me do that. Then, after a couple of months, I got real lucky. A bunch of shooters moved on to other jobs, and there I was as a full-time photographer."

Flexible and Undemanding

"The advice I would give somebody starting out in any aspect of television is that you have to be absolutely 100 percent completely flexible and undemanding for a long time just to get experience," says Michael Eskridge. "If you can get a job sweeping the floors in the smallest station in Oklahoma, with a chance to fill in once in a while helping out in the studio on the weekend programs, then do it. The hardest thing to get is the first job that gives you any experience."

"I think the advantages of working in small-to-medium-size markets are that you learn all the different things you can do with the equipment," says sportscaster Mark Olesh of Bakersfield's KERO-TV. "If you know fully what resources are at your disposal, there are a lot more avenues you can take to put together different types of interesting pieces.

"There's also a lot less pressure at those stations, and the opportunity to make mistakes without getting fired."

Ann Compton says, "Getting a little taste of everything and covering all types of stories is crucial to the development of TV journalists."

Terry Baker advises, "No matter what aspect of the business you're interested in, you should look for the place where there's the most opportunity to learn and grow—usually small markets—where you can go in as an untrained college graduate and two years down the road have a lot more skills and responsibility."

That's exactly what happened to Karen Horner. She was an English major without any newswriting experience when she got her first TV news job in Colorado Springs just a few years ago.

"That's where I started developing my own personal style, not just adapting to others," says Horner. "I had the opportunity to develop a more creative producing style—there was more creative license. And you develop more confidence because you quickly become the head honcho."

CBS sportscaster Greg Gumbel says he was fortunate enough to begin his career in Chicago—not exactly a small market. He says he had virtually no experience in the business, but that Chicago's WMAQ-TV gave him plenty of time to learn the ropes.

"The most important thing in this business [for those working on-camera] is to be seen by, and impress, a lot of people," says Gumbel. "That's a lot easier in a market like Chicago than a real small market somewhere."

He admits, however, that the chances for rookie sportscasters, or anyone wanting to work on-camera for that matter, of starting in a big market are slimmer today than ever before.

"Nowadays, there's very little tolerance in larger markets for learning. Smaller markets offer fewer pressures and give the novice a lot more latitude to learn and grown on the job by doing it all.

"On the other hand, news management can be a real obstacle at the local news level. If they want you to concentrate solely on local sports, it's hard to develop the necessary skills . . . and you can get stuck in small markets. So you should cover as much professional action as possible.

"Newcomers tend to work to please their bosses. You can't do just that. Of course you've got to take their wishes into consideration. But you've also got to do what works best for you. You need to work to please and benefit yourself, especially in the long run."

As for improving one's skills and moving up the ladder, Gumbel says, "I found the best thing to do is to look at your own work. I pick myself apart. I'll screen it and critique myself, and I think I'm the toughest critic I have."

Poor Pay

The pay in small markets, quite frankly, stinks. But the experience will carry you on to your next job smelling like a rose. The stiff competition just to get a foot in the door of TV news allows small stations to get away with paying their employees next to nothing. Remember, if *you* don't want the job, there are hundreds of others ready to step right in.

"The pay is going to be lousy—about $10,000 to $15,000 a year for most people just starting out," warns Rick Brown. "It's important to know that. You can't go into this business with the idea of making big money. That never happens for some people. So if the business isn't important to you for journalistic reasons, you're going to be disappointed."

Doing It All

It helps when you look for that first job to know specifically what role you want to play in the newsroom. Although you may not start out in that position, you can certainly focus your efforts in that direction. That means making it clear to your superiors what your goal is, and trying to show them every chance you get that you're worthy of the task.

But regardless of your title in the small-station newsroom, you're likely to become the proverbial jack-of-all-trades. Assignment editors and producers sometimes go out on stories with photographers, and reporters and anchors must sometimes cover the assignment desk and produce newscasts.

"In Wausau [Wisconsin], I'd go out with another reporter, I'd shoot his stories, he'd shoot mine, we'd edit all our own stories, and then I'd produce a newscast later," says Jodi Fleisig, who later moved on as a producer to Milwaukee, New Haven, New York, and Atlanta.

Lincoln Furber worked for twenty years as a newsman before becoming director of the broadcast journalism program at American University in 1977. In the May 1989 issue of the monthly magazine *Communicator*, published by the Radio-Television News Directors Association, he summed up the first reporting job in a small market:

"Reporters at most small-market stations think up story ideas, set up the interviews, carry the cameras, recording and lighting gear, operate the equipment, edit the videotape, write the copy and go on the air with the finished story. They can anchor and produce newscasts and public affairs programs as well as do sports and weather and participate in station-publicizing promotional activities. At times it can seem daunting and just too much. . . . But this is the 'experience' that it is possible to get in the small markets."

Shooting Yourself: The One-man Band

Indeed, reporters at some small stations even have to set up and shoot their own standups (live, on-the-scene reports of an occurrence). How do you do that? Although it isn't easy, nor is it preferable, the best way is to get someone else who's around, someone about the same height, if possible, to stand in front of the camera while you focus. Then, with the camera rolling, you grab the microphone, position yourself exactly where that person stood, and deliver your standup. If there isn't anyone around to help, focus instead on an object in that place and guesstimate how the shot should be framed with you in it. The guesstimating gets a little easier with experience.

Some broadcast industry experts venture to say that in this era of heightened budget consciousness and lighter, easier-to-use ENG equipment, the one-man band, (a reporter who shoots his or her own stories) will become even more common, especially in small markets and at regional cable news operations.

"The business is constantly changing," says Lou Prato. "I think we're going to see more mergers of TV stations in the future, resulting in fewer jobs and more one-man bands."

But at least for the time being, statistics show that the number of newspeople working at TV stations in small markets has remained largely unchanged in recent years. And staffs in medium markets have actually been growing. It's the stations in the top 50 markets, those with the largest staffs, that have done most of the cutting.

In 1991, the typical TV station (an average of stations big and small) had 22 full-time and three part-time staffers in the newsroom. The total TV news work force in the United States was estimated at somewhat more than 23,000.

Kinks in the Gear

Paying your dues at a small station can be highly rewarding. Because you're dealt so much responsibility, you can take a lot of credit when things go well.

But things don't always go as planned. The equipment in small markets is generally older than average, perhaps even a bit outdated, and prone to malfunctions. In addition, there may not always be an engineer around to work on broken-down cameras, tape decks, tripods, and editing machines.

Brace yourself for the occasional overwhelming feeling of disappointment and, in some cases, outright anger. Just when you're set to shoot some of the greatest video of the most exciting story to hit town in a decade, you may find that you can't record sound, or worse, the camera won't roll because of a short in the cable. Lo and behold, there's neither an engineer on duty back at the station to fix it nor a spare set of equipment to use. Many small stations stock only enough gear to cover a few stories at once, and several important events may occur simultaneously.

A photographer and I once captured some great footage of young children driving three-wheel all-terrain vehicles (ATVs) on the giant sand dunes near Yuma, Arizona. At the time, state and federal lawmakers were considering further restrictions on the use of ATVs. Because of a kink in the old tape deck, the bumpiness of the ride back to the highway was enough to trigger the rewind mechanism and spin the tape back to the beginning.

Not realizing what had happened, the photographer shot my next interview over the pictures of the ATVs. Because it was already late in the day, we didn't have time to make the long drive back to the dunes for more shots. And since the producer had already blocked off (reserved) two minutes for the story, we had to use some file footage we had stored back at the station, which showed only adults driving the vehicles. Needless to say, the story lacked a great deal of impact without shots of small children behind the wheel.

Frustrating? Indeed.

Human Error

And then there's human error, more common at small stations, but nevertheless lurking just around the corner at big shops as well.

One of my first live appearances on the set at CNBC was plagued by human error. After being introduced by one of the anchors with whom I briefly ad libbed, I turned to one of the cameras to read the introduction to my package, only to realize that the guy controlling the teleprompter had accidentally shifted the machine into reverse. Having never learned to read whole sentences as they move backwards off the screen, I knew I was in trouble. I did, however, manage to find my place on the hard copy in front of me and finish introducing the package.

I thought the worst was over. But not so. Nearly two minutes later, as we were chatting on the set while awaiting the end of my taped story, an audio engineer "opened" my mike (brought the volume back up on my microphone) several seconds before the package ended. The viewing audience clearly heard me asking the director which camera he wanted me to look at during the live tag to my story. (I should have confirmed that earlier.)

And as if all that wasn't bad enough, the floor manager in the studio forgot to cue me when the package ended. So I sat there on-camera for a couple of seconds (which in broadcasting seems like an eternity), waiting for a cue that never came. I glanced over at a monitor, saw that I was back on the air, and resumed reading. I couldn't help but feel embarrassed and a little bit foolish.

Early Rewards

The rewards and excitement, however, almost always outweigh the frustrations. The opportunities are great at small stations for any member of the news team to delve into a variety of interesting issues. You may find yourself uncovering political corruption one day, accompanying police on a big drug bust the next, and later in the same week exposing a rip-off artist at a local auto repair shop.

While working in Yuma, I investigated a telephone sales company peddling books of coupons, many to the elderly, filled with misleading information and a lot of fine print. We found out from the city that the company had never obtained a license to do business there.

The con artists involved vacated the motel room where they had set up shop before we were able to track them down. But the story we broadcast alerted the public to the problem, and the district attorney's office vowed to ban the company from operating in Yuma in the future.

The public response to the story was most favorable. Our station received dozens of phone calls and letters of praise, and I was stopped several times on the street by people who said they wanted to see more such stories. The experience was definitely a high point for all of us involved in breaking the story.

"When you start in a smaller market, the experience can be really exciting and a lot of fun," says Jodi Fleisig. "The people are hungrier and they're pushing harder. You're working with a lot of young, excited, ambitious people shooting for a common goal."

Thinking Better and Bigger

As I mentioned earlier, news directors often don't have, or make, the time to give you much advice on how to improve your work. Besides, you might find yourself at a small station where you know more about news than just about anyone else, including, in a few towns, the news director.

If the news director is able and willing to help you out, great. Take advantage of the input. But you can also learn a great deal by watching how others operate, especially your counterparts at bigger local stations and at the networks. In addition, send samples of your work to news directors or their assistants in larger markets who might critique it and keep you in mind for future job openings. Some will be willing to help. Others won't. But the more you try, the more likely it is you'll get back some valuable constructive criticism and build upon your list of important contacts. That's where the schmoozing comes in.

■ 6 ■
Picking Your Targets

There are more than 200 media markets in the United States, all with at least one news-producing TV station, and, most with three network affiliates (local, NBC, ABC, and CBS stations). Many of those cities are also home to independent, public, and a fast-growing number of local and regional cable TV operations that air news and public affairs programs of their own. A handful of companies have even developed 24-hour news and information services in New York City, Long Island, Boston, Washington, DC, Chicago, and Orange County, California. And with more channels in the works, cable TV will provide a growing number of news jobs in the years ahead. (See Arbitron's rankings of all media markets by size at the end of this chapter.)

Narrow Your Focus

Rather than indiscriminately applying to every station and spreading yourself awfully thin, begin your job search in a particular region of the country where you'd like to live and work.

For example, if you live in Los Angeles, you may want to start your search in California, Arizona, New Mexico, Nevada, and Oregon. Then, if you don't happen to be in the right place at the right time, you can expand your search to other areas.

Once you've chosen a region (and again, don't be too selective, because you can select yourself right out of a job) find and record the station's call letters, address, phone number, and network affiliation (if any), and the name of the news director of each station to which you plan to apply.

All of the information you need to know about broadcast and cable TV stations, and then some, is listed in a couple of annually updated publications. *Broadcasting & Cable Market Place* and *Television and Cable Factbook* are huge industry resources that can be found in many public and college libraries, and just about any television station. Because the books are expensive and contain much more information than you'll ever need for a job search, I don't recommend purchasing one. Search your local libraries and broadcasting stations first. Then, should you decide you want your own copy of one of the books, write or call

Broadcasting & Cable Market Place
1705 DeSales Street, N.W.
Washington, DC 20036
(202) 659-2340

Television and Cable Factbook
2115 Ward Court, N.W.
Washington, DC 20037
(202) 872-9200

Taking Note

Devote a separate sheet in a notebook to each station that interests you. You'll need room to jot down the date and brief descriptions of each conversation or correspondence you have with a news director. I tried index cards, but I ended up having to write in tiny letters on the back to keep a record of what was said and eventually ran out of space.

The notes will serve as a reminder of any constructive criticism the news director might have offered regarding your work, hints on when a job might open up at that station, and when to contact him or her again.

Don't Take It Personally

Some news directors don't like spending time talking to applicants, especially if the station has no openings at the time. Therefore, some sheets in your notebook are likely to remain blank. Don't be discouraged. It's probably nothing personal.

Rookies and seasoned pros alike must brace themselves for rejection. Some news directors simply don't mince words. During the search for my second on-camera reporting job, I sent a tape and resume to a station in the large Hartford–New Haven market. What I got back several days later was a brief note from the news director, who candidly wrote, "At this time, I don't think you have the skills and experience we are looking for in our current opening."

If that's not blunt, I don't know what is.

"In this business, more than in any other business, or certainly as much as in any other business, you've got to be prepared for rejection," says Marv Rockford.

Rejection is tough to take, but those searching for jobs in TV news must be mentally prepared for plenty of it. Don't take it personally. Hang in there. Often, what one news director dislikes, another admires.

"For most people," says Rockford, "if you're flexible in terms of what you're willing to do and where you're willing to go to do it—I mean very flexible in terms of geography—and if you're aggressive, you'll find work. You'll find a job."

Table 1
ADI Market Rankings, 1991–92

ADI Rank	ADI Market Name	ADI TOT HH	% TV	ADI TV HH	% of U.S.
1	NEW YORK	6,845,200	99	6,749,500	7.35
2	LOS ANGELES	5,007,000	98	4,883,200	5.32
3	CHICAGO	3,033,800	99	2,999,700	3.27
4	PHILADELPHIA	2,666,600	99	2,637,400	2.87
5	SAN FRANCISCO-OAKLAND-SAN JOSE	2,277,800	97	2,208,000	2.41
6	BOSTON	2,153,900	99	2,126,300	2.32
7	WASHINGTON, DC	1,791,400	99	1,781,100	1.94
8	DALLAS-FT. WORTH	1,777,100	99	1,763,400	1.92
9	DETROIT	1,733,000	99	1,719,100	1.87
10	ATLANTA	1,467,600	99	1,456,800	1.59
	1-10 TOTAL	28,753,400	99	28,324,500	30.86
11	HOUSTON	1,465,400	99	1,452,000	1.58
12	CLEVELAND	1,435,900	99	1,421,800	1.55
13	MINNEAPOLIS-ST. PAUL	1,394,600	99	1,380,100	1.50
14	SEATTLE-TACOMA	1,422,900	97	1,379,400	1.50
15	MIAMI-FT. LAUDERDALE	1,294,600	99	1,286,300	1.40
16	TAMPA-ST. PETERSBURG	1,253,500	99	1,243,000	1.35
17	PITTSBURGH	1,153,900	99	1,139,600	1.24
18	ST. LOUIS	1,124,000	99	1,110,900	1.21
19	SACRAMENTO-STOCKTON	1,080,800	97	1,045,700	1.14
20	PHOENIX	1,044,600	98	1,021,500	1.11
	1-20 TOTAL	41,423,600	99	40,804,800	44.46
21	DENVER	1,024,900	98	1,008,200	1.10
22	BALTIMORE	967,900	99	963,900	1.05
23	ORLANDO-DAYTONA BEACH-MELBOURNE	935,000	99	926,900	1.01
24	HARTFORD-NEW HAVEN	939,300	99	925,600	1.01
25	SAN DIEGO	935,400	97	911,200	.99
26	INDIANAPOLIS	863,800	99	853,200	.93
27	PORTLAND, OR	869,400	97	839,900	.92
28	MILWAUKEE	772,800	99	765,300	.83
29	KANSAS CITY	770,200	99	762,900	.83
30	CINCINNATI	767,300	99	759,000	.83
	1-30 TOTAL	50,269,600	99	49,520,900	53.95
31	CHARLOTTE	745,800	99	740,000	.81
32	RALEIGH-DURHAM	737,300	99	729,300	.79
33	NASHVILLE	724,500	99	720,900	.79
34	COLUMBUS, OH	699,000	99	691,300	.75
35	GREENVILLE-SPARTANBURG-ASHEVILLE	664,400	99	657,900	.72
36	BUFFALO	636,900	99	629,400	.69
37	GRAND RAPIDS-KALAMAZOO-BATTLE CREEK	619,900	99	612,700	.67
38	NORFOLK-PORTSMTH-NEWPORT NEWS-HAMPTN	612,100	99	607,500	.66
39	MEMPHIS	601,900	99	597,000	.65
40	NEW ORLEANS	600,500	99	595,400	.65
	1-40 TOTAL	56,911,900	99	56,102,300	61.12

Table 1 (*continued*)
ADI Market Rankings, 1991–92

ADI Rank	ADI Market Name	ADI TOT HH	% TV	ADI TV HH	% of U.S.
41	SAN ANTONIO	592,100	99	584,900	.64
42	SALT LAKE CITY	595,100	98	584,600	.64
43	PROVIDENCE-NEW BEDFORD	577,900	99	571,700	.62
44	OKLAHOMA CITY	569,100	99	564,900	.62
45	LOUISVILLE	553,600	99	549,700	.60
46	WEST PALM BEACH-FT. PIERCE-VERO BEACH	552,400	99	546,800	.60
47	HARRISBURG-YORK-LANCASTER-LEBANON	554,100	98	542,900	.59
48	GREENSBORO-WINSTON SALEM-HIGH POINT	531,700	99	527,400	.57
49	WILKES BARRE-SCRANTON	527,800	98	518,500	.56
50	BIRMINGHAM	507,900	99	505,100	.55
	1-50 TOTAL	62,473,600	99	61,598,800	67.11
51	ALBANY-SCHENECTADY-TROY	511,100	99	503,500	.55
52	ALBUQUERQUE	517,000	97	502,000	.55
53	DAYTON	503,700	99	498,900	.54
54	JACKSONVILLE	475,600	99	471,500	.51
55	CHARLESTON-HUNTINGTON	467,600	99	462,200	.50
56	FLINT-SAGINAW-BAY CITY	456,200	99	451,500	.49
57	LITTLE ROCK	455,100	99	449,100	.49
58	TULSA	447,800	99	443,600	.48
59	FRESNO-VISALIA	458,600	96	441,700	.48
60	RICHMOND	441,300	99	436,900	.48
	1-60 TOTAL	67,207,600	99	66,259,700	72.19
61	WICHITA-HUTCHINSON	427,100	99	423,200	.46
62	KNOXVILLE	424,200	99	420,900	.46
63	MOBILE-PENSACOLA	412,800	99	410,200	.45
64	TOLEDO	405,400	99	401,300	.44
65	ROANOKE-LYNCHBURG	393,300	99	389,300	.42
66	SYRACUSE	387,500	98	381,500	.42
67	GREEN BAY-APPLETON	384,400	99	380,700	.41
68	AUSTIN, TX	379,700	99	375,200	.41
69	PORTLAND-POLAND SPRING	375,000	98	368,800	.40
70	DES MOINES	371,200	99	368,000	.40
	1-70 TOTAL	71,168,200	99	70,178,800	76.46
71	SHREVEPORT-TEXARKANA	367,900	99	362,600	.40
72	ROCHESTER, NY	362,700	99	358,300	.39
73	OMAHA	359,900	99	356,700	.39
74	LEXINGTON	345,800	99	342,300	.37
75	PADUCAH-CP GIRARDEAU-HARRISBURG-MARION	338,800	98	333,000	.36
76	SPRINGFIELD-DECATUR-CHAMPAIGN	339,000	98	333,000	.36
77	SPRINGFIELD, MO	325,600	98	318,900	.35
78	TUCSON	317,300	98	311,200	.34
79	LAS VEGAS	315,900	98	310,700	.34
80	SPOKANE	319,800	97	310,000	.34
	1-80 TOTAL	74,560,900	99	73,515,500	80.09

Table 1 (*continued*)
ADI Market Rankings, 1991–92

ADI Rank	ADI Market Name	ADI TOT HH	% TV	ADI TV HH	% of U.S.
81	CHATTANOOGA	308,800	99	306,900	.33
82	CEDAR RAPIDS-WATERLOO-DUBUQUE	302,400	99	298,800	.33
83	DAVENPORT-ROCK ISLAND-MOLINE: QUAD CITY	301,300	99	298,100	.32
83	JOHNSTOWN-ALTOONA	303,600	98	298,100	.32
85	BRISTOL-KINGSPORT-JOHNSON CITY: TRI-CITY	298,200	99	295,100	.32
86	SOUTH BEND-ELKHART	299,400	99	295,000	.32
87	COLUMBIA, SC	293,000	99	289,100	.31
88	HUNTSVILLE-DECATUR-FLORENCE	287,800	99	285,400	.31
89	JACKSON, MS	279,100	99	276,100	.30
90	FT. MYERS-NAPLES	278,600	99	275,200	.30
	1-90 TOTAL	77,513,100	99	76,433,300	83.27
91	YOUNGSTOWN	272,100	99	269,300	.29
92	MADISON	269,500	98	265,200	.29
93	EVANSVILLE	262,400	98	258,200	.28
94	WACO-TEMPLE-BRYAN	252,900	99	250,200	.27
95	BATON ROUGE	252,300	99	249,500	.27
96	SPRINGFIELD, MA	251,800	98	247,700	.27
97	BURLINGTON-PLATTSBURGH	244,800	98	240,800	.26
98	LINCOLN-HASTINGS-KEARNEY	240,800	99	238,600	.26
99	COLORADO SPRINGS-PUEBLO	242,400	98	238,100	.26
100	EL PASO	240,700	99	237,800	.26
	1-100 TOTAL	80,042,800	99	78,928,700	85.99
101	SAVANNAH	235,100	99	232,000	.25
102	FT. WAYNE	234,600	99	231,500	.25
103	LANSING	228,800	99	226,300	.25
104	GREENVILLE-NEW BERN-WASHINGTON	228,100	99	225,900	.25
105	CHARLESTON, SC	226,100	99	223,100	.24
106	SIOUX FALLS-MITCHELL	220,600	99	218,600	.24
107	PEORIA-BLOOMINGTON	220,600	98	217,000	.24
108	FARGO	215,700	99	212,800	.23
109	SANTA BARBARA-SANTA MARIA-SAN LUIS OBISPO	217,100	96	209,000	.23
110	MONTGOMERY-SELMA	210,100	99	208,000	.23
	1-110 TOTAL	82,279,600	99	81,132,900	88.39
111	SALINAS-MONTEREY	215,800	96	207,900	.23
112	AUGUSTA	205,400	99	203,300	.22
113	TYLER-LONGVIEW-JACKSONVILLE	202,600	99	199,800	.22
114	MCALLEN-BROWNSVILLE: LRGV	199,600	99	196,800	.21
115	TALLAHASSEE-THOMASVILLE	198,100	99	195,300	.21
116	RENO	197,300	97	191,400	.21
117	EUGENE	199,000	96	190,300	.21
118	FT. SMITH	189,700	98	186,600	.20
119	LAFAYETTE, LA	183,800	99	181,600	.20
120	MACON	182,700	99	180,200	.20
	1-120 TOTAL	84,253,600	99	83,066,100	90.50

Table 1 (*continued*)
ADI Market Rankings, 1991–92

ADI Rank	ADI Market Name	ADI TOT HH	% TV	ADI TV HH	% of U.S.
121	COLUMBUS, GA	181,700	99	179,700	.20
122	TRAVERSE CITY-CADILLAC	182,900	98	179,500	.20
123	LA CROSSE-EAU CLAIRE	176,300	98	173,500	.19
124	COLUMBUS-TUPELO	172,300	99	170,100	.19
125	CORPUS CHRISTI	171,400	99	169,400	.18
126	DULUTH-SUPERIOR	170,500	99	168,200	.18
127	AMARILLO	167,300	99	166,000	.18
128	MONROE-EL DORADO	168,200	99	165,700	.18
129	YAKIMA-PASCO-RICHLAND-KENNEWICK	172,100	96	164,900	.18
130	CHICO-REDDING	167,600	96	161,600	.18
	1-130 TOTAL	85,983,900	99	84,764,700	92.35
131	WAUSAU-RHINELANDER	163,000	98	160,400	.17
132	BAKERSFIELD	163,900	97	158,600	.17
133	BINGHAMTON	160,800	98	158,300	.17
134	BEAUMONT-PORT ARTHUR	159,600	99	158,200	.17
135	ROCKFORD	157,000	99	155,000	.17
136	TERRE HAUTE	157,200	98	154,400	.17
137	SIOUX CITY	153,500	99	151,900	.17
138	FLORENCE-MYRTLE BEACH	153,100	99	151,000	.16
139	WICHITA FALLS-LAWTON	151,800	99	150,900	.16
140	ERIE	152,600	98	150,300	.16
	1-140 TOTAL	87,556,400	99	86,313,700	94.04
141	TOPEKA	152,300	99	150,100	.16
142	BOISE	152,300	98	149,000	.16
143	WILMINGTON	148,100	99	146,100	.16
144	WHEELING-STEUBENVILLE	143,900	99	142,400	.16
145	JOPLIN-PITTSBURG	139,800	99	137,900	.15
146	BLUEFIELD-BECKLEY-OAK HILL	136,500	99	134,800	.15
147	LUBBOCK	135,400	99	134,600	.15
148	ROCHESTER-MASON CITY-AUSTIN	135,700	99	134,400	.15
149	MEDFORD	139,900	96	133,900	.15
149	MINOT-BISMARK-DICKINSON-GLENDIVE	135,100	99	133,900	.15
	1-150 TOTAL	88,975,400	99	87,710,800	95.56
151	ODESSA-MIDLAND	134,400	99	133,400	.15
152	COLUMBIA-JEFFERSON CITY	134,600	99	132,600	.14
153	ALBANY, GA	133,600	98	131,400	.14
154	SARASOTA	130,300	99	129,300	.14
155	BANGOR	126,300	98	123,900	.13
156	QUINCY-HANNIBAL	109,900	99	108,700	.12
157	ABILENE-SWEETWATER	107,900	99	107,100	.12
158	BILOXI-GULFPORT-PASCAGOULA	107,100	99	106,600	.12
159	CLARKSBURG-WESTON	106,000	99	104,900	.11
160	IDAHO FALLS-POCATELLO	106,800	98	104,800	.11
	1-160 TOTAL	90,172,300	99	88,893,500	96.85

Table 1 (*continued*)
ADI Market Rankings, 1991–92

ADI Rank	ADI Market Name	ADI TOT HH	% TV	ADI TV HH	% of U.S.
161	UTICA	105,500	98	103,900	.11
162	PANAMA CITY	98,000	99	96,700	.11
163	SALISBURY	96,300	99	95,300	.10
164	LAUREL-HATTIESBURG	95,200	99	94,300	.10
165	GAINESVILLE	91,600	98	90,000	.10
166	DOTHAN	89,700	99	88,900	.10
167	HARRISONBURG	89,000	99	88,000	.10
168	WATERTOWN-CARTHAGE	87,700	99	86,400	.09
169	ELMIRA	88,000	98	86,300	.09
170	PALM SPRINGS	88,800	97	85,700	.09
	1-170 TOTAL	91,102,100	99	89,809,000	97.84
171	RAPID CITY	86,100	98	84,600	.09
172	BILLINGS-HARDIN	86,300	97	84,000	.09
173	ALEXANDRIA, LA	84,700	99	83,600	.09
174	LAKE CHARLES	81,200	99	80,400	.09
175	GREENWOOD-GREENVILLE	75,100	98	73,700	.08
176	JONESBORO	72,900	98	71,800	.08
177	MISSOULA	73,300	97	71,300	.08
178	ARDMORE-ADA	70,400	99	69,500	.08
179	GRAND JUNCTION-DURANGO	69,500	97	67,400	.07
180	EL CENTRO-YUMA	71,300	94	67,300	.07
	1-180 TOTAL	91,872,900	99	90,562,600	98.66
181	MERIDIAN	65,700	99	64,900	.07
182	GREAT FALLS	63,400	97	61,800	.07
183	JACKSON, TN	57,900	99	57,400	.06
184	PARKERSBURG	57,400	99	56,600	.06
185	TUSCALOOSA	56,300	99	55,900	.06
186	MARQUETTE	56,800	98	55,700	.06
187	EUREKA	55,700	96	53,400	.06
188	SAN ANGELO	49,400	99	48,900	.05
189	ST. JOSEPH	49,500	98	48,700	.05
190	BUTTE	50,100	97	48,600	.05
	1-190 TOTAL	92,435,100	99	91,114,500	99.27
191	BOWLING GREEN	46,300	99	46,000	.05
192	HAGERSTOWN	45,500	99	45,200	.05
193	LAFAYETTE, IN	46,000	98	45,100	.05
194	ANNISTON	43,200	99	43,000	.05
195	CHEYENNE-SCOTTSBLUFF (STERLING)	42,200	99	41,600	.05
196	CHARLOTTESVILLE	41,400	99	40,800	.04
197	CASPER-RIVERTON	40,700	98	39,800	.04
198	LIMA	39,500	98	38,900	.04
199	LAREDO	38,600	98	38,000	.04
200	TWIN FALLS	36,300	98	35,600	.04
	1-200 TOTAL	92,854,800	99	91,528,500	99.72

Table 1 (*continued*)
ADI Market Rankings, 1991–92

ADI Rank	ADI Market Name	ADI TOT HH	% TV	ADI TV HH	% of U.S.
201	OTTUMWA-KIRKSVILLE	33,900	99	33,600	.04
202	PRESQUE ISLE	31,200	98	30,500	.03
203	ZANESVILLE	30,900	98	30,400	.03
204	MANKATO	30,300	99	29,900	.03
205	FLAGSTAFF	31,400	94	29,400	.03
206	BEND	30,000	95	28,500	.03
207	VICTORIA	26,200	98	25,800	.03
208	HELENA	18,900	97	18,300	.02
209	NORTH PLATTE	17,600	99	17,500	.02
210	ALPENA	16,200	97	15,700	.02
	TOTAL U.S. TV HOUSEHOLDS	93,121,400		91,788,100	

Source: The Arbitron Company.

ADI = Area of Dominant Influence
TOT HH = Total Number of Households in Area
TV HH = Total Number of Households with TVs

∎ 7 ∎

Job Services and Publications

Whether you're looking for your first job in television news or you've already put in some time, it may well be worth your while to invest a little money in periodicals and services designed to help in the search.

Phone Service

MediaLine is a popular telephone service that frequently surveys TV stations in every media market and is often the first to publicize job openings. By subscribing to MediaLine, you receive a telephone number and code that allow you to listen to recordings updated daily with some of the latest job openings around the country. The messages tell you who to contact at particular stations, and what materials to send.

The service offers a variety of recordings for different types of TV news, production, and promotion jobs, so you don't waste your time and long-distance calling money listening to a lot of voice mail you don't need. There's even a separate entry-level jobs recording.

MediaLine, albeit indirectly, helped me land my second TV news reporting job. After I subscribed in 1988, the service listed an opening at KRDO-TV in Colorado Springs for a weekend anchor who would also report from the field three days during the week. It was the same type of job I had worked my way into in Yuma, but in a bigger market. I applied. The news director told me he liked my reporting, but he said I didn't look "mature enough" for the weekend anchor job. I guess at age 29, I still needed a few more gray hairs and lines on my face.

Although I didn't get that job, the news director said he thought enough of my work to keep my tape on his "top shelf" for future consideration. A few months later, however, he and a reporter took jobs elsewhere, leaving the new news director, Jeff Thomas, with a reporter slot to fill. He saw my tape and resume and called me in Yuma to see whether I would be interested in the position. I, of course, said yes, though I candidly told him I had another job possibility in the works as well.

When it rains it pours. I had just returned from a successful interview at a station in Albuquerque, New Mexico, where management told me that I was among the final two candidates being considered for a reporter job. I was excited about the prospect of working for that station, under a highly respected news director whom I had already come to know during my first job search.

Nevertheless, in our second phone conversation in as many days, an enthusiastic Thomas came right out and offered me the job in Colorado Springs. He said he needed an answer pronto and gave me the weekend to think about it. I immediately called Albuquerque, where instead of dragging me along, the news director kindly admitted it would be another two or three weeks before a final decision was made.

I figured a bird in the hand in this business is worth about a million in the bush. After discussing the issue with my wife, who had attended college in Colorado Springs and liked the area, I called Thomas and accepted his offer. Although Albuquerque is the larger of the two cities (albeit not by much), Colorado Springs had the reputation of being more active and a good stepping-stone to Denver and other top markets. Besides, the beauty and quality of life in "The Springs," nestled at the foot of Pikes Peak, are hard to match.

The bottom line is that if I had not heard about the original job listing on MediaLine, I might never have applied to KRDO-TV in the first place. The service isn't cheap, but it's a terrific resource that may give you a head start.

Publications

Trade magazines can also prove to be helpful in finding a job. You can find one of the most extensive job listings in the weekly magazine *Broadcasting*. The publication includes openings in all areas of television and radio news and entertainment.

Electronic Media, another weekly magazine, has a slightly smaller classified section but focuses solely on television. It also does an excellent job concisely covering trends and innovations in the industry.

Many TV stations receive *Electronic Media* and *Broadcasting*, and they may allow you to stop by and look through a few issues. If that doesn't work, check your local libraries, newsstands, and bookstores. Subscriptions are expensive, but the investment may be worthwhile. Perhaps you can split the cost with others looking for jobs.

If you're serious about a long-term career in the business, you'd be well-advised to join the Radio-Television News Directors Association (RTNDA). Twice each month RTNDA members receive the newsletter *Intercom*, which focuses on current issues facing the industry. It's accompanied by a job bulletin listing dozens of openings, with space to advertise your own skills and availability at a nominal cost.

The RTNDA also sends out to members a monthly magazine, *Communicator*, which focuses on the latest technology and trends in broadcast news. The knowledge gleaned from trade journals can help you score points with news directors as you discuss particular news operations, techniques, and the industry in general.

In addition, the RTNDA has set up a special phone line that provides frequent updates on job openings.

Going beyond the Ads

You may be asking yourself what good it will do to subscribe to the same services and publications that so many other applicants are using in their job searches. It's true that many job hunters subscribe to these services, but don't let the numbers discourage you. Your job search would probably be tougher without the help of such resources, though it would be a mistake to rely solely on them.

Contact all the news directors at stations in the area you've targeted, even if no job openings have been posted. Because the turnover rate in small markets is quite high, you may hit a news director at a time when a member of the staff has just resigned or announced his or her intention to do so. That's the luck factor in this business. But you can make your own breaks by working as hard at the job search as you will on the job. Once again, *persistence* is the key.

News directors must keep a balanced staff and often know when they post job openings whether they'll hire a man or woman, and whether he or she will be a minority. Although equal opportunity hiring laws prevent them from advertising along racial or sexual lines, news directors often hint at the type of person they're looking for with such sayings as "Wanted, anchor for weekday newscast to complement male anchor." That usually means they're looking for a female anchor, since most stations use male-female anchor teams. "Minorities encouraged to apply" may be another hint that news directors are looking for a particular type of person (i.e., a minority candidate, to fill the job).

Many of the ads in broadcast industry publications say the employer is looking for someone with experience. They often state a minimum number of years required, though most news directors remain a bit flexible on that issue—depending, of course, on the talent of the applicant. Other job openings are listed as entry-level positions. Employers—especially in small markets, where the pay isn't enough to attract more-experienced candidates—understand that one's eagerness and hard work can make up for a lack of experience.

Why Not Hire an Agent?

Many news veterans hire agents, or headhunters, to help them find, and negotiate for, well-paying jobs in big markets. They look for someone with a good track record who they're confident will represent their best interests. Most prefer to work with an agent who doesn't get paid until they do.

But with few exceptions, those of you just starting to climb the ladder must rely on your own job-finding skills. "Agents are a useful tool later on, but even then they're not miracle workers," says Marv Rockford. "Nobody can negotiate a great deal for you unless you've got leverage, and most people who have just come out of school have no leverage. Most people in their first couple of jobs have no leverage. An agent in those situations isn't going to be able to get any more money for you, certainly not enough extra money to pay for his or her fee. In fact, it's probably going to cost you money."

San Francisco–based agent Jean Sage agrees that representing beginners is a no-win situation. "I'm not interested in anybody until they've had at least three years in the business. Not until then will I look at their writing, their ability to put together a strong package, and their ability to communicate well. They should be ready for the top 20 or 30 markets, or the networks. Otherwise, the low salaries don't warrant using an agent."

Summary of Job Sources

Here are some of the services and trade publications that will likely prove helpful in your job search:

MediaLine
P.O. Box 51909
Pacific Grove, CA 93950-6909
(800) 237-8073 (outside California)
(408) 648-5200

Also ask about the MediaLine RTNDA Update, a special telephone call-in service for RTNDA members only. It includes job listings updated every Monday, Wednesday, and Friday.

To join the Radio-Television News Directors Association, which includes the monthly *Communicator* magazine and the semimonthly *Intercom* newsletter and job bulletin, write to or call

RTNDA
1000 Connecticut, Suite 615
Washington, DC 20036
(202) 659-6510

If you don't wish to join the RTNDA but would like to get the semiweekly job bulletin or advertise your own availability therein, contact

RTNDA Job Information Service
c/o National Television News
23480 Park Sorrento, Suite 201
Calabasas, CA 91302
(818) 883-6121

The RTNDA Job Updates number is (900) 40-RTNDA (75 cents per minute at the time of publication of this book).

Don Fitzpatrick Associates runs a telephone job service that is updated daily called The Pipeline. There is no membership fee. But as with the RTNDA Job Updates service, the cost of dialing the 900 telephone number is likely to exceed the cost of making a regular long-distance call. So use it judiciously. The Pipeline number is (900) 456-2626.

For more information on The Pipeline contact

Don Fitzpatrick Associates
Ghirardelli Square, D-404
900 North Point
San Francisco, CA 94109
(415) 954-0700

If you are interested in trade magazines, contact these publishers.

Broadcasting
1705 DeSales Street, N.W.
Washington, DC 20036
(800) 638-SUBS (toll-free subscription line)
(202) 638-1022 (main office)

Electronic Media
740 North Rush Street
Chicago, IL 60611
(800) 678-9595 (toll-free subscription line)
(312) 649-5200 (main office)

The National Association of Broadcasters runs a department designed to encourage the hiring of minorities and women in broadcasting. For information contact

Director of Employment
Clearinghouse, National Association of Broadcasters
Minority and Special Services Department
1771 N Street, N.W.
Washington, DC 20036
(202) 429-5355

If you're looking for an on-camera TV news job, it can't hurt to send a copy of your audition tape and resume to the following news consultants.

These companies are paid by various stations to help improve the quality of their newscasts. And they're always looking for talented people to recommend to those stations. It may be a long shot, but you can't beat the cost—there's no charge to you other than postage.

Audience Research & Development
c/o Placement Services
8828 Stemmons
Dallas, TX 75247
(214) 630-5097

Frank N. Magid Associates
One Research Center
Marion, IA 52302
(319) 377-7345

Don Fitzpatrick Associates
Ghirardelli Square, D-404
900 North Point
San Francisco, CA 94109
(415) 954-0700

∎ 8 ∎
The Resume

First Impression

Your resume will probably be the first thing a news director looks at when you apply for a job. That first impression is crucial. A news director who likes your resume will probably read your cover letter and look at your audition tape. But a news director who is not impressed with your background and the way you've presented it on paper probably won't look any further.

Resumes can be drawn up in many styles, but certain rules of thumb should be applied.

Eye-catching Layout

Keep it to one page. At the top of the page, use bold letters for your name, followed by your mailing address and phone number in normal print. Making your name stand out will help news directors spot it more quickly on their cluttered desks and remember it more easily. Bold letters, perhaps just a touch smaller than those used for your name, should also be used to highlight job titles, education degrees, and other distinctive parts of your resume.

The layout should be eye-catching, yet simple, concise, and easy to skim. The news director should be able to pick up the salient points at a moment's glance.

"News directors are very, very busy people, or at least they think they're very busy, which I guess amounts to the same thing," says Marv Rockford. "So they're going to spend very little time with you and your resume. One page of very direct, easy-to-understand information is best—about who you are, where you've come from, and what you've done. It's got to be something you can scan, and in scanning pick up the essential information very quickly."

Some people use their own computers to produce attractive resumes. Others go to print shops where resumes can be typeset by professionals in a variety of styles. Whichever method you choose, it's always advisable to use high-quality stationery, including matching envelopes.

Work Experience

Unless you're just out of school with no journalism or related background, Work Experience should be the first category on your resume. Start with your current or most recent job or internship and work backward chronologically. A line or two should suffice to succinctly describe your responsibilities in each position. Further explanation can be included in the cover letter if necessary, though that too should be written concisely. Be sure to list where you worked and when you worked there. It is also appropriate in the work experience category to list jobs you've had that were unrelated to journalism, staying with the reverse chronological order. Many news directors look for well-rounded applicants.

Education

Only if you've had no experience in journalism or communications in general but have earned a degree in a related field should you make Education the first category on your resume. This is especially true if you attended a school with a solid reputation. Generally, the smaller the market, the less work experience is required, and education may become the most important criterion.

Put yourself in the seat of a news director. Decide which of your experiences are most impressive and qualify you for the job.

For those who list work experience first on the resume, education should follow, and vice versa. List the academic degree, or degrees, you've earned, and where and when you earned them. If you're enrolled in college and applying for part-time work or an internship, be sure to name the school and your major.

News directors generally don't care where you went to high school, unless you're still there or you recently graduated, or you attended one near a small station to which you're applying. Familiarity with an area can be a plus and may deserve mention in your cover letter.

Miscellaneous

What you put after work experience and education is much more up to your own judgment. I've always titled this category Miscellaneous; some people call it Personal. It's a good place to devote a few lines to outstanding achievements, honors, interests, hobbies, or just about anything else that might set you apart from the rest.

You are under no obligation to list your age, marital status, or ethnic and religious background. In fact, federal law prevents employers from discriminating on that basis. You should only mention one or all of the above if you think it will help you land a job.

On my resume, for example, I include the fact that I'm married. I've heard some news directors say that shows you have a sense of commitment. The theory is that you're not as likely to leave after only a few months if you have a spouse and his or her career to think about as well.

And at a time when stations are trying to keep an ethnically balanced staff, it certainly can't hurt to let a news director know if you're a minority candidate, especially if minorities have been encouraged to apply.

References (Last, but Not Least)

The final category on your resume should be References, and it's a must. List the names, titles, and phone numbers of two to four people with whom you've worked, preferably superiors in the broadcast news field or journalism teachers. A single line should suffice for each. Title abbreviations for your references are OK.

Make sure the people you choose as references know you well enough to speak highly of your abilities and potential in electronic journalism. Don't bother to list their addresses. The news director won't have time to write to them for comments. You'll be lucky if he or she picks up the phone to call any of them. (But if this happens, it usually means you have a real shot at the job. So make sure the phone numbers are all current.)

If you're already working in TV news and have an open and honest relationship with your news director, and if you're confident this person will vouch for your character, then you can list your current boss as a reference. Who better to speak of your abilities? But if you're conducting your job search more discreetly, as is often the case, don't include your current news director as a reference.

Some news directors are supportive of efforts by members of their staff to move up to bigger markets; others aren't. You've just got to follow your gut instincts on this one.

I was lucky. News director Jeff Thomas promised when he hired me that if I gave him "one good year," he'd fully support my efforts to move on. Each of us fulfilled our end of the bargain.

Don't list as references fellow workers or acquaintances who might also be in the job market, perhaps looking for similar jobs. That's a situation that can backfire and result in the reference getting hired, making enemies of friends.

Take my friend Len Johnson, for example, now a weatherman in Baltimore. He listed a fellow reporter in Yuma as a reference on his resume. But when the news director at a station in Florida called her to ask about Len, she reportedly turned the conversation toward her own experience and abilities. She quickly sent that news director a resume tape, and she, not Len, got the job. So take note. It's a fiercely competitive business. Select your references very carefully!

Boasting the Truth

Again, give your most valuable experiences big play on the resume, making sure they stand out. There's nothing wrong with making it appear boastful. The purpose of a resume is to let the news director know why he or she should hire you over all the others.

But be truthful. Don't exaggerate. News directors are a smart bunch. They can see through little white lies and may ask you to further explain the jobs, education, and other experiences you've listed. They may also ask you to account for missing periods of time on your resume.

According to a recent survey published in *Communicator*, vice-presidents and personnel directors at top American corporations cited the biggest flaws they've found in applicants' resumes:

Problem Cited	Percentage
Distortions/Lies	36%
Too Long	36%
Errors/Misspellings	21%
Lack of Specifics	19%
Irrelevant Material	11%
Failure to List Job Accomplishments	19%
Too Short	2%

Source: Burke Marketing Research.

The following are copies of my own resume and that of John Daenzer, who recently got his first full-time job in the business as a producer. Both layouts are eye-catching, though they differ substantially.

JEFF LESHAY

2536 McDaniel Avenue
Evanston, IL 60201
W: (312) 555-3016
H: (708) 555-5035

WORK EXPERIENCE

CORRESPONDENT, CNBC, Chicago/New York
Cover business, consumer and environmental issues for daytime and primetime.
Feb. 1990–Present

REPORTER/ANCHOR, KRDO-TV, Colorado Springs
Covered government, environment, military and general news. Filled in frequently
as anchor. Jan. 1989–Feb. 1990

REPORTER/ANCHOR, KYEL-TV, Yuma, AZ
Won nine AP Broadcasting Awards, including first place in investigative, general and
series reporting. Anchored and produced weekend newscasts. Sept. 1987–Jan. 1989

BROADCAST WRITER/EDITOR, The Associated Press, Hartford
Wrote and edited copy on state and local politics, business, police and fire, features
and sports. Oct. 1986—July 1987

WASHINGTON CORRESPONDENT, WIBW-TV, Topeka
Localized national stories during final quarter of graduate program, Medill School
of Journalism. June–Sept. 1986

STRINGER, The Associated Press, Manila Bureau, Philippines
Reported on anti-government demonstrations. Feb.–March 1985

ASSOCIATE PRODUCER, Financial News Network, Santa Monica, CA
Produced and wrote early morning news. Jan.–Aug. 1984

PROFESSIONAL TENNIS INSTRUCTOR, Vic Braden Tennis Colleges,
Germany, Universal City Racquet Centre, CA June 1980–Aug. 1985

EDUCATION

M.S.J., BROADCASTING
Medill School of Journalism, Northwestern University. Sept. 1986

B.A., HISTORY
University of California, Santa Barbara. March 1981

MISCELLANEOUS

BILINGUAL: French. Lived in France and England, 1971–75.
French professional tennis circuit, 1979. Varsity tennis, U.C.S.B.
Age: 34 Married

REFERENCES

Jamie Avery, Producer, CNBC, Fort Lee, NJ (201) 555-2622
Jeff Thomas, News Director, KRDO-TV, Colorado Springs (719) 555-1515
Rick Brown, Graduate Instructor, Northwestern (708) 555-2561
Lou Prato, Director, Medill News Service, Washington, DC (202) 555-8700

John C. Daenzer

7908 Amber Rd.
Fort Wayne, IN 46804

219/555-3915

OBJECTIVE
- Full-time position or paid internship as a television news writer or producer

EXPERIENCE

Summer 1992 — *National High School Institute - Journalism, Northwestern University*
- Instructed high school students in television news production; broadcast writing; news writing and reporting; feature writing, and in-depth reporting and writing.

Spring 1992 — *WNUR Radio, Evanston, Ill.*
- Wrote news stories and anchored weekly newscasts
- Produced field reports for weekly newscasts

Spring 1992 — *Evanston Stories, Evanston, Ill.*
- Reported, wrote and edited packages for this cable news magazine

Spring 1991 — *Albuquerque Journal, Albuquerque, N.M.*
- Reported and wrote general assignment stories
- Edited news copy and wrote headlines
- Daily Circulation: 130,000

Summer 1989,
Summer 1990,
Summer 1991 — *Fort Wayne Journal-Gazette, Fort Wayne, Ind.*
- Wrote feature stories for a regional supplement
- Wrote high school sports stories
- Covered *NCAA Division I* college sports
- Daily Circulation: 64,000

Winter 1989
to Winter 1990 — *The Daily Northwestern, Northwestern University*
- Wrote feature, news and police stories
- Daily circulation: 9,100

EDUCATION

Medill School of Journalism, Northwestern University
- Bachelor of Science in Journalism degree, June 1992
- Course concentrations in Broadcast Writing, Editing and Producing; Political Science; Slavic Studies and African-American Studies
- Placed 10th nationally in the *William Randolph Hearst* sportswriting competition
- Cumulative Grade Point Average: 3.33/4.0

COMPUTER AND VIDEO EDITING SKILLS

Trained to use:
- *New Star II* newsroom computer
- Sony Hi-8 and 3/4" video camera
- Sony Hi-8 and 3/4" video editing equipment

ACTIVITIES

Northwestern University, Evanston, Ill.
- Sole student Organizer "*Operation Spruce-Up 1990*," a student volunteer effort to paint Chicago Housing Authority apartments
- Executive member in charge of production for *CCI Publishers, Inc,* a student corporation that now publishes a campus-wide, student telephone directory and advertising section
- Volunteer for *Northwestern Volunteer Network* adult literacy tutoring program
- Vice President for Academic Affairs, *Residential College of Commerce and Industry*
- Bible discussion leader for *InterVarsity Christian Fellowship*
- Member of the *Northwestern University Singers* ensemble

John C. Daenzer

7908 Amber Rd.
Fort Wayne, IN 46804

219/555-3915

REFERENCES

Academic

Professor Bob Mulholland, Broadcast Program
Director
Medill School of Journalism
1845 Sheridan Road
Evanston, IL 60208
(708) 555-2090

Ed Planer, Adjunct Lecturer
Medill School of Journalism
1093 Linde Lane
Glencoe, IL 60022
(708) 555-1139

Professor Brenda Boudreaux
Medill School of Journalism
1845 Sheridan Road
Evanston, IL 60208
(708) 555-1314

Professional

Professor Roger Boye, Director
National High School Institute - Journalism Division
1845 Sheridan Road
Evanston, IL 60208
(708) 555-2069

Mr. Phil Bloom, Outdoors Editor
Fort Wayne Journal-Gazette
600 W. Main St. P.O. Box 88
Fort Wayne, IN 46801-0088
(219) 555-8260

■ 9 ■

The Cover Letter

Why Hire You?

The cover letter can help you make up for lack of experience or formal education. It's an opportunity to tell the news director why you want the job, how eager you are to learn, and how motivated you are to succeed.

Some news directors won't even read your cover letter, at least not thoroughly. Others will. There's no telling who will and who won't. So put as much effort into writing a strong cover letter as you put into every other aspect of the application process.

Although this may be your only chance to explain how you can contribute to the news team, keep it short and on one page. Concisely tell the news director the type of job for which you are applying, and why you are interested.

"The whole point being you have to give it all to him very, very quickly," says Marv Rockford. "I see a lot of letters that come across my desk from people looking for jobs, and they write very long, eloquent cover letters that I don't have any time to read."

You may want to discuss briefly how your experiences have prepared you for the job. But don't merely reiterate what you've included on your resume. Let your personality flow onto the paper. Tell the news director why you should get the job. Explain how hard you're willing to work. There certainly are some people in the business who have gotten by on good looks, but very few who haven't worked hard to succeed.

Like the resume, the cover letter should be a little boastful yet retain a touch of humility. The first job or two can be very humbling, and you need to emphasize your willingness to do just about anything to help the station succeed.

Sports and weather jobs tend to be more entertainment oriented than those in news. If you're interested in sports or weather, gear your letter accordingly. Show a bit of charm or flare, and perhaps a touch of humor. But don't lose sight of the other necessary ingredients.

Cut the Malarkey

Don't waste the news director's time by including such trite phrases as "I want to work in Palm Springs because I like the clear, sunny skies all year long," or "I want to work at your station because I adore the town." That's malarkey! You may indeed love the area, but the news director knows you want the job for the very reason that it's a foot in the door and quite possibly a stepping-stone to a larger market. The director was once, and in fact may still be, in a similar situation.

Having relatives or other close ties to a town may be worth mentioning, but only if you really believe it'll give you an edge. Jeff Thomas took such factors into account when he hired a sports anchor who had been working in Waco, Texas, over a couple of other equally talented applicants. Thomas says he based the decision in part on the fact that the guy he hired had often visited relatives in Colorado Springs and was already familiar with sports in the region.

Write to the Point

Keep your sentences short and conversational, demonstrating the appropriate broadcast writing style. The cover is likely to be the first sample of your writing the news director sees, though the writing of reporters, anchors, and producers should shine through on the audition tape as well.

There are some excellent how-to broadcast writing books on the market. Four that I have found most helpful are

Writing News for Broadcast by Edward Bliss, Jr., and John M. Patterson, Columbia University Press, 1978.

Writing Broadcast News — Shorter, Sharper, Stronger by Mervin Block, Bonus Books, 1989.

Rewriting Network News: WordWatching Tips from 345 TV and Radio Scripts by Mervin Block, Bonus Books, 1990.

TV News Off-Camera: An Insider's Guide to Newswriting and Newspeople by Steven Zousmer, University of Michigan Press, 1987.

These are the kind of books to keep and refer to throughout your career.

Make No Mistake

Check the cover letter again and again for typos or other mistakes. Then have someone else with good literary skills look them over. You can never be too careful when it comes to applying for a job in this detail-oriented business.

Handwritten changes look sloppy; retype the whole page if necessary. Make your cover letter and resume look *perfect*.

News directors receive dozens, often hundreds, of applications for each opening. Don't give them the excuse they're looking for to throw yours in the "circular file" as they narrow down their list of candidates.

The following are copies of the cover letter I sent to CNBC's executive producer Peter Sturtevant when I won a reporter job at the cable network, and the cover letter that accompanied John Daenzer's resume (seen at the end of chapter 8).

Jeff Leshay
3332 Quail Lake Road, #212
Colorado Springs, CO 80906
(719) 555-1186

December 12, 1989

Mr. Peter Sturtevant
Executive Producer
CNBC
2200 Fletcher Ave.
Fort Lee, NJ 07024

Dear Peter:

I'm a nose-to-the-grindstone reporter who leaves no stone unturned. My stories are clear, thorough and accurate, and my serious approach to newsgathering would contribute greatly to the CNBC news team.

My strongest asset is that I truly care about the news. That's because I subscribe to the philosophy that a fully and accurately informed public is best able to govern itself wisely. I enjoy working with others toward a common goal, and I'm willing to put in long, hard hours to produce high-quality pieces. My wife will attest to that.

Given the opportunity, I'll prove you made a correct decision in hiring me. Thanks for your time and consideration.

Sincerely,

Jeff Leshay

Jeff Leshay

October 3, 1992

John C. Daenzer
7908 Amber Road
Fort Wayne, IN

Les Vann, News Director
WICS-TV 20
Springfield, IL

Dear Mr. Vann,

My name is John Daenzer, I'm a news junky, and I want to work for WICS as a news producer. I'm excited by television news, I'm challenged by daily deadlines, and I understand broadcast writing's power when it is carefully matched with video.

I recently graduated from the Medill School of Journalism at Northwestern University. While a student, I developed a strong news background in several newsrooms, and I have produced my own television and radio news shows.

I will be in Springfield on October 15. I would like to visit your station to meet with you. I will call you on October 10 to verify that you received this letter and hopefully to arrange a time for us to meet. I look forward to speaking with you soon.

Thank you for your time and consideration.

Sincerely,

John C. Daenzer

John C. Daenzer

▪ 10 ▪
The Audition Tape

Putting Your Best Work Forward

The audition tape, or resume tape, is an all-star lineup of your best work. It's a videotape record you send to news directors that shows how well you can report, anchor, write, produce, shoot, or edit.

Audition tapes are rarely, if ever, needed when applying for internships. Those who hire interns usually don't expect them to have much, if any, hands-on TV news experience. But news directors looking to fill full-time jobs will often place much more emphasis on audition tapes than on other criteria.

Few reporters, anchors, photographers, or videotape editors are hired without audition tapes. On-air personalities hired from radio, however, have been known to get by with samples of their work on audio cassettes. Producers sometimes get their first TV news jobs based on writing samples in the form of scripts. But they too stand to benefit if they can provide an audition tape demonstrating the best show or segments they've helped get on the air.

Anyone who hasn't worked with professional TV news gear can use home video equipment to put together a tape. If nothing else, it shows initiative.

Assignment editors generally don't submit audition tapes, since their behind-the-scenes news managerial work may not be apparent on the air. However, the demonstration of organizational and leadership skills and good news judgment is crucial, whether exercised in TV, radio, or print journalism. Therefore, news directors rely much more heavily on the resume, cover letter, and most important, the interview when looking to hire an assignment editor or news desk assistant.

Working as an intern or in another entry-level position is probably the best way to put together your first audition tape. You can seek technical help from the station's staff and tap the news managers for guidance in writing, reporting, shooting, editing, or anchoring stories. You may have to work on the tape after hours, but it'll be time well spent.

Seldom do stations allow interns to report stories on the air. However, it does happen from time to time, and one should take full advantage of such opportunities. Writers, shooters, and editors should also keep their eyes and ears open for any chance to make the airwaves. You can't beat that kind of experience and exposure.

Much of the following advice on building audition tapes is applicable across the board to anyone vying for a job in television news. Although the formats differ, common threads bind them, and each method provides insight for another.

Reporters: Letting Them Know Who You Are

During the search for my second reporter job in TV news, I experimented a little, structuring my audition tapes in a number of different ways. A couple of months and dozens of tapes into the search, I found a method that seemed to leave a greater impression with news directors.

I had gleaned from talking to many news directors that they want to hear and see prospective reporters right away. Some have even been known to fast-forward audition tapes past the top story, or part of it, to a point where the reporter appears on-camera.

"News directors are going to want to see fairly early in the tape what you look like," my first graduate broadcast instructor, Rick Brown, told me.

So to avoid having them overlook my favorite story, I began my tapes with two or three of my better standups, back-to-back. The opening standups I used were pulled from packages other than those I would include further along on my tape, so as not to be repetitive. A brief montage of stand-ups immediately satisfies news directors' natural curiosity to see the person to whom they're listening.

"I like the standup montage off the top," said one assistant news director in Des Moines who kindly took the time to critique my tape during my second job search. "It gives me a good idea who I'm dealing with." Unfortunately, he also said I needed more experience for the reporting job he was looking to fill.

News directors don't want to see standups for the sake of standups—those which neither advance the story nor add anything of value to it, and appear to be done merely to get the reporter's mug on TV. What they do want to see, whether in a montage of standups at the beginning of the tape or in the packages, is someone comfortable on-camera, smoothly delivering valuable information from a location relevant to the particular story.

And just to show that there are exceptions to every rule of thumb in this business, it's important to mention that a few news directors are critical of using even a quick montage of standups at the top of the tape.

"Opening with a bunch of standups or liveshots [live reports from the field] doesn't tell me about a reporter, to be honest," says Terry Baker. "Those should be givens. Every reporter should be able to do those things. I want to see good writing and hear good questions that need to be asked. I want to see stories with good, solid reporting. You need something special. What is often missing is the coming up with creative story ideas."

Showcasing the Right Stories

Following a quick montage of standups, or alternatively, right at the beginning of the audition tape, reporters should hit the news director with a few of their best packages. The stories should be well-written and edited, enhanced by a strong and effective voice. Open with your most impressive package.

If you're applying for a general assignment reporter job, which means covering breaking stories, like police and fire emergencies, politics, and features, you should include different kinds of stories on your tape. Starting with a good breaking news story or two catches the news director's attention and shows you can cover events quickly and thoroughly. Then break up the pace with an interesting feature piece.

"The good news director wants to see something special in terms of human interest, reporting style, a variety of hard news and features," says Rick Brown, who advises job applicants to include three to five packages on the audition tape. "Show them diversity. Show them you're well-rounded."

If a station needs to fill a particular type of reporting job that you're interested in, such as a political or health reporting slot, tailor your tape accordingly. Make sure to start with your best political or health story first. That may well be the only piece the news director sees. Remember, news directors usually have dozens of tapes to look through. They simply don't have time to watch all those stories. More often than not they determine within the first few seconds whether you're still in the running for the job. But if they like the first story, they're likely to keep watching.

Keeping It Tight

Make sure the writing in all packages is tight. Most stories shouldn't exceed a minute and a half, and many news directors prefer general assignment–type stories not to exceed one minute and twenty seconds. Special features or important breaking news might be a little longer. But keep in mind that conciseness is of the essence. News directors like to get as many interesting stories on the air as possible. The theory is that fast-paced, action-packed newscasts won't bore the viewers.

I happen to think many stories warrant more than a minute and a half on tape and are interesting enough to hold the viewers' attention. But that viewpoint is typical for reporters, who are constantly pushing for more time to tell their stories.

The need to demonstrate sharp writing skills in the news stories you submit on the tape is exactly why you should read and practice the broadcast writing techniques shown in a number of books on the market (see chapter 9). Those books explain how to minimize the number of words you use while maximizing their effectiveness. And they focus on the use of active verbs to make stories as exciting for the viewers as they were for you to witness firsthand.

Working Your Voice

Reporters and anchors should use their voices, though quite subtly, to help convey the excitement, sadness, seriousness, or other emotions associated with particular stories. Most important, one's voice should be clear, authoritative, and easy to listen to.

Rick Brown says voices can be made stronger with practice. But not all voices, he candidly adds, are well suited for broadcasting.

"Many people just aren't blessed with a very good, strong voice. Some can overcome that. Some can't. The voice is not as important for the first job in a small market. The problem comes after the first job. But those people with weaker voices shouldn't give up on TV news. They can be good producers."

Two books especially helpful in learning to use one's voice effectively in broadcasting are *The Voice as an Instrument* by Raymond Rizzo, MacMillan, 1978, and *Broadcast Voice Handbook: How to Polish Your On-air Delivery* by Ann Utterback, Bonus Books, 1990.

Frivolous Openings

Back to the audition tape itself. Some people like to launch their tapes with a several-second countdown or color bars. Either is fine, though neither is necessary. But forget including countdowns or color bars between packages. Just a bit of "black" will do.

"A nice quiet, subdued second or two of 'black' in between cuts on the tape is a must—no countdowns please," wrote San Francisco–based news consultant Don Fitzpatrick in *Communicator.*

Color bars are used by engineers to check audio and video balance. But when put between stories on a tape, they, like a countdown, serve no purpose in the news director's office other than to waste time.

Another option is to use a graphic slate at the top of the tape showing your name, address, and phone number. Some people even use graphics to introduce each segment on the tape. I happen to think those too are a waste of time. All that information can be listed clearly in an index on the tape box.

Graphics may look sharp, but they merely reflect the capabilities of the machinery used to make them, not your own skills. There are those who argue that quick, imaginative graphics, such as the turning of a page introducing each segment, add a touch of class to the tape. That may be. But keep in mind that they won't make up for any shortcomings in the stories themselves, which remain the bottom line for most news directors.

Some reporters and anchors go so far as to start their tapes by introducing themselves on-camera, much to the dismay of many news directors and consultants.

"Each time I see talent open his or her audition tape sitting in an edit booth or in the newsroom with: 'Hi, I'm Jane Doe and I want to be your reporter. . . ' I tune out," wrote Fitzpatrick.

For anchors show opens are also frivolous. The following remarks illustrate Fitzpatrick's dim view of them: " 'And now the newscenter for the greater mountains and lower seas of the western world presents the news at 6:00 with Brad Blowdry and Brenda Buxom anchoring, Jacque Strap on Sports and Stormin Wormon with the accurate weather. And now, Brad and Brenda . . . '

"Are we hiring the graphics company that puts together the show open? No! Hopefully we're going to see a tape from Brad, Brenda, Jacque or Stormin. But we certainly don't need to waste another 30 seconds of the news director's time watching a prepackaged show open. The only thing worse would be to see a 30-second promotional spot that the station did on the talent. More waste of the news director's time. Again, he/she is not going to hire the advertising agency."

Sandra Connell of Audience Research & Development says, "Sports and weather folks can get away with some added creativity," though she admits she's only been impressed by a couple of show opens out of the many hundreds she's viewed. "It isn't necessary for anchors or reporters." However, she adds, "I do want to see some personality [during the newscasts]. "

The way you put together your audition tape can literally make or break your chances of getting a job.

"Many talent audition tapes are poorly constructed and many of those tapes have lost their owners jobs," says Fitzpatrick.

The following are some of the biggest mistakes, from most common to least, Fitzpatrick says he and fellow news consultants come across when viewing audition tapes.

Problem Cited	Percentage
Color Bars/Tone on Head of Audition Tape	80%
Show Opens to Intro Newscast	60%
Change of clothes after Each Story Read (Anchors Only)	50%
On-air Bios ("Hi, I'm Bob Smith and I want to work for your TV station!")	35%
Voice-over Bios	15%
Anchor/Reporter Sending Only Anchor Work	10%

Source: Don Fitzpatrick Associates.

High Impact

Remember, news directors want to see your own work right away. They'll probably hit the eject button on the machine if you haven't sold yourself in the first 30 seconds.

"The resume tape should be designed to have the highest impact in the shortest amount of time," says Marv Rockford. "That's the best advice I can give people. Take the best thing that you've got, and put it as the very first piece on your tape. What everybody has heard about news directors looking at a tape for no more than 30 seconds is absolutely true. Most news directors will make a judgment within 30 seconds about whether they like you or not, about whether they think you are employable or not. So if you don't have something that hooks them in that first 30 seconds of your very first piece, you've lost him."

In fact, the entire audition tape should move at a quick pace, as should an entire newscast. Hit the news director hard; grab that person's attention right away with powerful opening shots and sharp, catchy writing. Then compel the news director to keep watching. Don't let your target get away.

"Hit 'em, hit 'em, and hit 'em again. Don't let 'em breathe," says Jodi Fleisig.

Getting Attention Creatively

Rockford likes to tell the following story about a reporter he hired who came up with an unorthodox yet innovative way of compelling him to watch her entire audition tape:

"We have a number of people here [KCNC-TV] who we found and we culled from the stack of unsolicited tapes. And there's one reporter in particular who started off her audition tape with essentially a bloopers reel of herself, screwing up standups and in other funny situations.

"I'd been looking at audition tapes for an hour or so, looking at these very dreary tapes, and all of a sudden this one pops up with genuinely funny stuff—with outtakes from her work. And I watched it. I was chuckling and watching and at the end of it—that went on for about two minutes or so—she said, 'OK, now that I have your attention, let me show you what kind of work I can do.' Then she went into a series of very hard-hitting, hard-news pieces, because that's the kind of reporter she is. I was very impressed, and we ended up hiring her.

"The point is this woman understands how to grab my attention and compel me to watch. If you can't compel the news director to watch your resume tape, you're not going to be able to compel the audience to watch your pieces, or your newscasts if you're a producer."

Using Just the Right Shots

The sequencing of shots in stories is also important. The same assistant news director who told me he liked the montage of standups at the beginning of my tape said I hadn't used enough medium and close-up shots in one of my stories. The package focused on the struggle by the Yuma Boys and Girls Club to survive with reduced funding from the city.

"Remember the basics: Wide shot/medium shot/tight shot," he wrote. "Look at the story on the activity center. All we see are wide shots of kids painting, wrestling, playing basketball, the library, cooking, pool, video games, back to the kitchen, and then a wide shot of a city council meeting."

He was right. And whether you're submitting an audition tape as a reporter, producer, editor, or photographer, using a variety of different types of shots and angles makes stories much more interesting and dramatic.

"Even for getting your first job, the basic shooting of wide, medium, and close-up shots is really important," says John Mason. "And those shots have to be steady. Whenever possible, photographers should shoot off a tripod. Sometimes you have to go hand-held [shooting off the shoulder, without a tripod] in breaking news situations, but even then a tripod is preferable."

No one knows that better than those whose job it is to edit the shots together.

"You need to make every shot count for something," says veteran editor Bart Cannistra. "Each shot should make a point relevant to the story. Wide shots should last long enough to show the details and context. A push in [of the camera] or close-up shot can then be used to highlight one of those details, causing the viewer to look at something specific, something important to the story. Another option is to have the camera pull out from something specific to reveal a relationship or secondary subject and put the whole thing in context.

"Whenever the camera moves, it should be for a reason. If the camera moves from one point to another, from A to B, it should be to show the relationship between A and B. Movement just for the sake of movement doesn't work. There's nothing worse than what I call aborted expectation—when the camera moves in one direction but never finishes, never comes to a stop. That can be the fault of the editor for not letting the shot finish before taking [editing in] the next shot, or it can be the fault of the photographer for not having finished the camera move in the first place [before focusing on something else]."

The following are informative books often recommended in college broadcast journalism courses because of their focus on TV news techniques. They include tips on editing, photography, writing, producing, and reporting that can help make your audition tape stand out.

ENG: *Television News and New Technology* by Richard Yoakam and Charles Cremer, South Illinois University Press, 1989.

Basic TV Reporting 1: Media Manuals by Ivor Yorke, Focal Press, 1990.

Interviews that Work: A Practical Guide for Journalists by Shirley Biagi, Wadsworth Publishing, 1992.

Writing to Pictures

Another constructive criticism of one of my early audition tapes included the following noteworthy advice from a news manager: "Use your copy to explain what we are seeing. Do not use video to cover over your copy."

In other words, write to the pictures. Good advice indeed, though one should never exclude important information just because there isn't a shot to clearly depict that element of the story. That's done too often in TV news. What you can't show can usually be said by the reporter in a standup, or by the anchor in the introduction or tag to the story.

The Buck Stops Here

Regardless of whether you shoot, write, report, anchor, produce, or edit the material on your audition tape, many news directors will hold you 100 percent responsible for all editorial and technical aspects of the work samples you submit. So choose your pieces very carefully.

Ask others you work with for their opinions on particular stories. A variety of feedback may get a little confusing, but you may find common criticisms among the remarks. Contemplate those comments seriously, and listen to your gut instincts. News directors are a fickle bunch and, like your peers, may view the same story in many different ways.

"News directors are enormously different in what they see as good," says Rick Brown. "And news directors have various levels of talent too— they're not all geniuses."

And while their tastes may differ, no news director likes to see static or other interference on the audition tape. So make sure you send out high-quality copies of your stories.

"It's important to have it technically clean," according to Brown. "News directors can get distracted by even minor technical problems and subtly blame you, even if it's not your fault."

Going Live

Many small-market stations don't have the capability to air live reports from the field. But reporters, anchors, and shooters who've been lucky enough to do liveshots should include an impressive sample or two on the audition tape.

Reporters can use an exciting liveshot in place of a montage of standups at the beginning of the tape. But that's only advisable if the report was done at the scene of a breaking story, and if the station to which one is applying is equipped with the technology to broadcast live from the field.

Liveshots from the field give reporters the opportunity to show that, under pressure, they can smoothly deliver or ad lib quickly gathered information without reading from a script or giving the notepad more than an occasional glance.

Shooters who have captured compelling live video at the scene of an unfolding news story or sports event should consider leading their tapes with that footage (with narration by a reporter or anchor included). It's exciting to watch, and also, news directors want to know whether you can capture powerful pictures in a hurry.

"You need to start your resume tape with exciting spot news, whether the piece aired live or on tape," says John Mason. "That's just my philosophy. Anybody can spend three days putting together an impressive feature story. I think news directors want to see how well and how quickly you can work under pressure.

"Because news directors' desks are packed full of tapes, you really need something that is going to stand up and grab people, especially at the beginning. It's got to be something different, something incredible. It can't be a plain tape or it's not going to go anywhere.

"And one other thing," Mason adds. "Working with a good reporter makes a big difference in the way the piece is written and sounds."

It's true that good reporters bring to light the best work of photographers. But it works the other way too. Good photographers provide reporters, producers, and videotape editors with the kind of compelling shots necessary to create packages as interesting to watch as they are to listen to.

Photographers and reporters who don't open their audition tapes with coverage of breaking news, but who want to demonstrate their ability to "go live," may include a smooth liveshot or two in the middle of the tape to break up a string of packages, or at the end for a strong finale—that is, if they're confident the news director will get that far.

Anchors with an exceptional liveshot to show off should include it at the end of the tape, so as not to interrupt the flow of their best newscasts. Many news directors do like seeing their anchors report live from the field once in a while. It adds credibility.

Reporters Who Also Want to Anchor

Those of you who are applying for reporter jobs but would eventually like to try your hand at anchoring should include a few minutes of anchoring at the end of the audition tape. News departments rely on reporters to fill in on the set from time to time.

If you haven't anchored on the air, but have taped a mock newscast at school or during an internship, use that material on your audition tape. It will at least give the news director a hint of your anchoring potential.

If the job you're after entails a combination of reporting and anchoring, include your strongest suit first on the tape. Applicants more confident in their reporting abilities should start their tapes with a few packages, perhaps preceded by a quick montage of standups, or a liveshot, and followed with several minutes of anchoring. Those who feel better about their anchoring skills should open with some on-set work and afterward present a couple of strong packages and maybe a liveshot.

The Anchor's Tape

If it's a full-time anchoring job you're seeking, it only makes sense to lead your audition tape with at least several minutes of anchoring. But because even full-time anchors in many small and medium markets spend some time working in the field, applicants for those jobs should follow their anchoring with one or two strong packages, and if available, a liveshot.

"[It] makes the talent look shallow when a tape arrives with only anchoring clips," says Don Fitzpatrick. "Even if the anchor has done limited reporting, we need to see some reporting."

As for the anchoring itself, most news directors prefer to see several stories read during a single newscast. That demonstrates the anchor can maintain a high level of professionalism for a prolonged period of time. Editing together the best bits and pieces of anchoring from different newscasts only tells the news director you probably can't make it through a single show without screwing up. Besides, most news directors I know aren't fashion-conscious enough to care whether they see you in a variety of clothing.

If, however, you don't think the excerpts from one newscast offer enough samples of your reading, there's nothing wrong with including stories from a second show as well.

Eliminate from your tape the stories read by others during the newscast. Include only your reading of top news stories, perhaps a soft, cutesy story or two, and a little on-air "happy talk" with a co-anchor, weatherperson, or sportscaster—all during the same one or two newscasts, and in chronological order.

The Sports Reporter's Tape

Sports reporters, like news reporters, may want to begin audition tapes with a quick montage of standups or liveshots from the field—that is, if those elements are particularly strong. The three to five packages that follow, or that are used by some sports reporters to kick off the tape, should be upbeat, entertaining, and filled with the thrills and agony that characterize organized sports. Clever scripts, written to complement the video and natural sound, are a real plus. And a little humor or sarcasm can add color to your stories.

One sports reporter I know got his first job in Colorado Springs by incorporating a unique talent into his work at a college TV station. He drew caricatures of athletes and included them in his stories. The news director who hired him saw an opportunity to spruce up the station's "Athlete of the Week" segments. Instead of awarding plaques to the winners, the station honored them with amusing illustrations of themselves in action.

Because many small and medium stations keep a total of only two or three people in the sports department, many sports reporters move to the sports anchor desk on weekends and fill in occasionally during the week. So, sports reporters should include a little in-studio anchoring—either in the middle of the audition tape, to break up a string of packages, or at the end. Being able to handle anchoring responsibilities substantially increases the marketability of sports reporters.

The Sports Anchor's Tape

Full-time sports anchors, on the other hand, should open their audition tapes with just that—sports anchoring. Once again, sharp writing and delivery is crucial, and many news directors prefer to see a whole sportscast rather than excerpts from several different ones. That shows them you can maintain the necessary level of excitement and make few or no mistakes throughout an entire sportscast.

Since most sportscasters produce their own material, news directors also look at how you structure several minutes of sports information, what your priorities are, how well your words complement the video, and how smoothly you make the transitions between stories.

Just as sports reporters must be able to produce and anchor, sports anchors need to show that they can cover events in the field. For that reason they must be sure to include two or three strong, colorful packages on the audition tape following one or two of their sportscasts from the anchor desk. For those who've had the opportunity to report live from the field, a particularly strong liveshot or two may also be included in the mix.

Mark Olesh says maintaining "a high energy level throughout the tape [in both the anchoring and reporting segments] was really important in getting my job. The news director here [KERD-TV] really liked that, even though a few others thought it was too loud and that I should be more subdued. They all have different opinions."

Because it's so difficult to tell what news directors will like and dislike, Olesh and other sports anchors and reporters advise that you rely on your own intuition. Again, let your gut instincts dictate which exciting samples of work to include on your audition tape.

The Weather Tape

Aspiring weathercasters should demonstrate at least a working knowledge of meteorology and, perhaps most important, the ability to comfortably convey the information with a bit of pizzazz. Two or three creative performances in their entirety should do the trick.

"People applying for weather jobs must also be able to demonstrate on their tapes that they can interact well with the other people on the set," says Terry Baker. "They've got to show a lot of personality, and that they're personable."

Occasionally, small-market stations hire and train weathercasters based on personality and appearance alone. Whether experienced or not in the science of meteorology, a weathercaster must be able to translate complicated weather patterns into simple, straightforward information. Many viewers are interested only in determining the type of clothing they'll need to wear, and whether they should bring their umbrellas. The rest, some say, is entertainment.

"News directors have told me that so many weathercasters look the same and present the information in the same boring way," says weatherman Len Johnson of Baltimore's WBFF-TV. "After looking at a lot of audition tapes sent to my news director in Reno, I saw their point. I tried to put myself in their shoes, and I figured they'd want to see something a little different.

"So on my audition tape I took the chance to be different. I didn't even use any weather information in the first three minutes of my tape. I figured I had to grab the news director's eye right away."

What Johnson did was open his audition tape with a weathercast he'd done in Reno, Nevada, immediately following a rainstorm. He used a zany combination of videotape shot outside and special effects to describe, among other things, the smell of some dew shown dripping off a tree.

"I wanted to show them how the weather smells," says Johnson. "Everybody loves the smell after a rainstorm. But I'd never seen a weathercaster talk about it. I knew it would be different. Some news directors didn't like it. Others did."

Weathercasters with likable, colorful personalities often find success in the business. Take Dave Bender, for example. He spent less than a year at a station in Yuma before jumping right into the San Diego market. It didn't hurt Bender to have a helpful, high-ranking friend with a lot of clout at the San Diego station. But others who know him say his audition tape was hilarious and pulled its own weight.

One of the highlights of the tape featured Bender giving the national weather forecast as he walked around on a giant map of the United States he'd drawn on a dirt lot next door to the station. The scene was shot from above on the station's roof. It worked beautifully. Viewers laughed about it for weeks.

Now Bender is laughing. He's at Fox's WTTG-TV in Washington, DC, the seventh biggest media market in the country.

"But always get a second opinion on wacky stunts before putting them on your audition tape," cautions Johnson. "Some work and some don't.

"To be effective, you need to be yourself. You need to get the information right, but you need to have fun and be colorful while you're doing it.

"The advice is simple. Try to think when you're around your friends about what makes them laugh, and what makes them your friends in the first place. Then, try to be that way when the camera is pointed at you. And if you are that way, news directors will like it and people will tune in."

The Producer's Tape

News directors say good producers are especially hard to come by. What they're looking for are people who can use strong and creative writing skills to put together informative, compelling newscasts.

"Writing ability and pace are the two key elements in producing," says Rick Brown. "The pace has got to be strong and steady, with writing that's sharp and clear."

Entry-level candidates without producing experience must rely most heavily on writing samples and the interview to get them on the right track to producerhood. Those who have any experience in producing, or helping to produce, newscasts, even if just in school or during internships, should showcase that work on tape.

Like reporters and photographers, producers can grab a news director's undivided attention right away with a riveting liveshot at the head of a newscast, perhaps from the scene of a major crime, fire, or political event. That demonstrates the ability to coordinate and convey up-to-the-minute coverage of a breaking story, all the while making the split-second decisions necessary to prevent disruption of the rest of the newscast.

And in order to fully evaluate producing skills, most news directors want to see on the audition tape an entire newscast produced by, or at least with considerable help from, the job applicant.

Commercials should always be left out and replaced with just a fraction of a second of black to keep up the pace and hold the news director's attention. Weather and sports segments, usually written and edited independently of the news producer, can be cut as well and replaced with a split second of black.

Some news directors, however, prefer to see all portions of the show including weather and sports (but not commercials). Since their preferences vary widely, try to find out in advance what each news director is looking for. If you're unable to do so, include the whole shebang—news, weather, and sports. Better safe than sorry.

"I prefer to see the entire newscast to get a better sense of the flow and the overall content, packages and all," says Rick Brown. "I can always hit fast-forward and zip ahead. But other news directors don't want to sit through the whole half hour. It's one of those things that can be done in a lot of different ways. You've got to do what feels best for you."

What felt best for Karen Horner was to include on her audition tape a newscast that could have been extremely boring, but which she had worked hard to spruce up and make interesting.

"It's important to be able to do that, because every day isn't full of breaking stories," says Horner. "You can make it exciting with good writing, good video, and the use of interesting graphics."

Tosses, or segues, read by the news anchors leading into and out of the weather and sports segments should always be included on a producer's tape. Some of them are not only written by the producer but show where he or she placed those elements in relation to the rest of the newscast. Producers should also include teases before commercial breaks to demonstrate their sharp, catchy writing and use of tantalizing video to keep viewers tuned in.

"You've got to write terrific teases. They've got to be sexy. They've got to be promotable," says Jodi Fleisig. "If I don't grab my viewers in the first ten seconds of the program, I lose them. I can almost hear the click, click, click—the changing of the channels."

To supplement the audition tape, producers may accompany their application materials with copies of a few of their most clever scripts used in newscasts. News directors may or may not request separate writing samples. But that's all many beginners have to offer. And most of those heading newsrooms in small markets realize that not all people looking to break into producing have already had the opportunity to produce newscasts, whether at another TV station or in school.

Even in the search for her second producer job in the business, Horner says she was asked to include plenty of writing samples in addition to her audition tape.

"Channel 2 [KWGN-TV in Denver] said, 'Send every script you ever wrote,'" she says. "I sent them about 100 scripts, trying to include a lot of information that was right up-to-the-minute when I wrote the stories. I also sent them copies of teases I wrote. It's so important to be able to write good teases to stories."

The Right Specs

With the exception of producers, who ideally submit an entire newscast on tape, applicants for TV news jobs should try to keep the length of the audition tape to between 9 and 15 minutes. Remember, you'll be lucky if the news director watches more than 30 seconds of it. But news directors who really like your work will keep watching. And if they want to see more, they'll call and ask for it.

Whenever possible use airchecks on your audition tape. An aircheck is the professional copy of a story made by the station as it broadcasts the news. Not only does the dubbing of an aircheck onto your audition tape prove that your story actually aired, but the graphics superimposed on the screen during the airing of a story help identify interviewees and locations.

Different stations use different types of videotape. It's generally safe to send samples of your work on three-quarter-inch tape. Even though many stations have switched to the newer, half-inch ENG equipment (i.e., the Sony Betacam and Panasonic MII systems), almost all news directors still have access to three-quarter–inch viewing machines. But to be sure, contact the news director's office and find out which type of videotape he or she would prefer to receive. Use VHS tape only as a last resort. It may work well at home, but the quality just isn't as good.

Stations at which you've interned or schools at which you've studied broadcasting are the obvious places to build, and make copies of, your audition tape. If you don't have access to their machines, or to someone who does, you may need to pay a professional videotape service for help. That can be expensive and is therefore all the more reason to stay in contact, and on good terms, with the people who helped you during an internship or at school.

TV journalists already working in the business, but looking to move to a bigger market, usually put together audition tapes very discreetly in their spare time, late at night or very early in the morning.

Tapes Galore

You may be wondering where you can get hold of a plentiful supply of not-too-costly videotapes. Those of you without access to used tapes no longer needed by a TV station should contact a group called Carpel Video. The company recycles and sells tapes, guaranteeing them to be "broadcast quality." And the more you buy, the cheaper they are. So if possible, buy them in bulk with others who are also looking for jobs. Tapes can be ordered from Carpel Video by calling the company's toll-free number (800) 238-4300.

Laborious Labeling

All audition tapes and their protective boxes should be clearly labeled. Type (do not write) your name in block letters, followed by your address and phone number on small, white adhesive labels or blank index cards. Taking the time to type the information shows professionalism and pride in your presentation. Put one label on the front of the tape, another along the side you can see as the tape is being put into a playback machine, and another on the side of the tape box so the news director can quickly identify it in a pile on his or her desk or sitting on a shelf.

The front of the tape box is reserved for an index card, or similarly sized piece of paper, with the same information the other labels contain and an index listing the name and running time of each segment on the tape.

The following fictional example would work well for someone applying for a general assignment news reporter job.

JANE SMITH
155 Maple St.
Po Dunk, NY 12345
(212) 555-4321

Stand-up montage :35 (running time)

Stories reported:
  Bus Accident—school bus crashes in river 1:28
  Toxic Waste—found on beach 1:39
  V.P. Visit—campaign comes to town 1:35
  Rip-off—auto mechanic cheats drivers 1:30

Liveshot from the scene of a double homicide 2:10

The tape of someone applying for an anchor job that would also entail some reporting might look like this.

JOHN DOE
2121 Orange St.
Boon Dock, CA 54321
(818) 555-1234

Anchoring excerpts from single newscast 10-17-92 6:15

Packages:
  Layoffs—local factory trims down 1:35
  Lotto Winner—single mom on welfare 1:29

Liveshot from apartment building fire 2:15

And the following would be a suitable format for someone applying for a photographer position.

SEAN LEE
1357 Berry Dr.
Barn Yard, IL 01234
(312) 555-6789

Factory Strike—violence breaks out   2:30
Tornado Damage—picking up the pieces   1:45
Football Champs—high school team wins state   1:35
Disabled Artist—Vietnam vet paints from chair   1:55
Hazardous Waste—illegal dumping in river   1:41

The index helps the news director quickly find what he or she is most interested in seeing on the tape. Remember, put the index on the tape box, not on the tape itself. It's impossible to read a listing on the tape when it's rolling in the machine.

Make viewing your tape as easy and exciting as possible for the news director. A poorly put-together audition tape can knock you out of the running right away. A professional-looking tape, as neat on the tape box as it is compelling on the screen, can win you the seat you want in the newsroom.

▪11▪
Applying for the Job

Quick Reactions

As soon as you find out about an appealing job opening, immediately send a cover letter, resume, and audition tape to the news director (unless, of course, the ad states otherwise—some news directors request only a resume at first, though that implies a cover letter as well).

There's no time to waste. So it's important to have plenty of resumes ready to go at a moment's notice. Although your cover letter and audition tape may need to be altered a bit to fit the requirements of a particular job, you should keep the stationery and tapes you'll need on hand.

Sending the materials first-class should get them to the station in time, and using an eye-catching "Priority Mail" envelope, available at the post office, may help draw attention to the packet. Such packaging exudes a sense of urgency that is lacking with ordinary white or brown envelopes.

If you learn that an especially attractive job opening has been posted for a while, consider spending the extra money to send your materials via an overnight delivery service. It may turn out to be a wise investment. If the news director is on the verge of making a decision, you want to make sure your work gets seen before he or she makes the final call.

Regardless of which mail service you use, the cover letter and resume should be neatly folded and slipped into a matching letter-size envelope addressed to the news director. That envelope should then be attached to the audition tape with a rubber band, and those materials put into the larger envelope. The purpose of addressing the smaller envelope is to make sure the news director gets the materials even if the larger one is opened by someone else at the station. The smaller envelope also protects the cover letter and resume.

Spraying the Markets

Once you've selected a region of the country where you'd like to work, spray the markets with cover letters and resumes, even if you don't know of any job openings there. At this point there's no need to send a tape. Follow up a week or so later with a phone call to the news director to make sure he or she received your materials, to reiterate your interest in working for the station and to find out if there are any openings in the foreseeable future.

But take note. Never, *never* call a news director close to news time. That's when chaos descends on the news room and the news director is called upon to make important last-minute decisions. News directors expect you to know that. I've had the most success telephoning them in the middle of the day—late in the morning after their story meetings, or early in the afternoon before all hell breaks loose.

If you're unable to get the news director on the phone, leave your name and number. Repeat the process until you get him or her on the line. That shows *persistence*, which most news directors appreciate as an integral part of journalism, though they might find it a bit annoying at times. It shows how determined you are to work in TV news.

Constant Reminders

If the news director seems at all interested in you, offer to send a tape, saying you'd appreciate any feedback or constructive criticism. If you're looking for a job in a larger market as a newswriter or production assistant, offer to send writing samples. The news director may tell you that you shouldn't send any more materials, but merely keep in touch, and that "we'll keep your resume on file" for future review. If that's what he or she says, take the advice. But try to touch base every few weeks via phone and mail.

Remember, the turnover rate in small markets is quite high, as people move on to bigger and better jobs after a year or two. Chances are if there's nothing open at a small station when you first establish contact with a news director, something will open up soon.

Other Helpful Hints

If applying for an on-air job, the inclusion of a photograph with your resume certainly can't hurt if you're exceptionally good looking. But those of us who are not that fortunate and bank more on our journalistic abilities should forget the photo. Send it to your mother instead.

Perhaps most important, invest in a telephone answering machine or service if you don't already have one. News directors may not try to contact you more than once or twice before focusing their attention on other candidates. More often than not they must fill openings very quickly.

■ 12 ■
Road Trips: Selling Yourself in Person

The Personal Touch

Once you've sent out your resume materials, establishing face-to-face contact with news directors can give you a competitive edge. You must become more than just another name on tape, and the only way to do that is by traveling to the station. For most people that means hitting the road.

Few people, especially those just beginning a career in TV news, can afford to fly to various towns in search of a job. And while road trips will likely mean many hours, even days, in a car, you may well find the extra effort to be worth your while.

"I think road trips are the most important thing," says Lou Prato. "That personal touch is most important. Nothing beats the one-on-one meeting where it's chemistry."

Not Taking No for an Answer

The trick is to convince a news director to set aside a couple of minutes to sit down and talk with you. Some news directors frequently take the

104

time to do that. Others don't like to conduct interviews when they don't have any openings. Others won't even see job applicants when they *do* have an opening until they've narrowed down their list of candidates by screening the large number of audition tapes they've no doubt received.

Don't take no for an answer. Be *persistent*, like a good reporter. Set up as many interviews as possible before you hit the road. Don't ask news directors *if* they have time to see you. That gives them a chance to say no. Tell them you plan to be in town, and ask *when*, not if, they'll have "just a couple of minutes" to see you. Again, some news directors will spend a little time with you; others won't.

If you can't set up an appointment with a particular news director, show up on the doorstep anyway once you get in town. What have you got to lose? Tell the receptionist or whoever greets you how far you've traveled. The news director may still decline to see you, but at least you've demonstrated *persistence* and can leave a tape and resume at the front desk. If nothing else, the news director will be more likely to remember your name and be a bit more cordial to you the next time you make contact.

Make the most of the time and money you spend on the road. Try to see *all* the news directors in the cities you visit and in other towns on your way there and back, even at stations where there are apparently no openings. At least you'll let them know who you are and how much a job at that station would mean to you.

Roughing It

Chicago-based cameraman Jeff Wierus, who does most of his shooting for ESPN, tells a great story about how he got his first job in the business.

Wierus had held several internships during his college days at Southern Illinois University in Carbondale and sent out about 150 resumes upon graduation. He says he got back 40 rejection letters and never heard from the other news directors.

"But I wasn't about to go home to Chicago after four years of school without first getting a job," says Wierus. "I realized that I'd have to make face-to-face contact at the stations. So a friend of mine and I got a bunch of resumes and tapes together and plotted all the markets and stations we wanted to go to."

Given their tight collegiate budgets, however, and the need to make their road trip affordable, these two aspiring electronic news gatherers bought a guide to campsites in the Southeast and packed an old Ford Escort with food, a tent, and sleeping bags.

"We actually had a great time," says Wierus. "We stayed on campgrounds with decent facilities, so we could shower and throw on a suit and tie in the morning, before heading over to the stations. We would always call the news directors at those stations the day before we'd get into town to let them know we'd be there.

"Finally, after ten days on the road, I got a job shooting in Charleston, South Carolina. The news director was impressed with the effort. If I had just sent a resume, and maybe a tape, it wouldn't have done anything. Without a doubt [the road trip] got me the job."

Wierus was only making $11,000 a year plus overtime. But he often worked 55 hours a week or more and says he "lived like a king in Charleston."

As for his camping buddy, well, that's another story. Wierus says he wasn't as fortunate in his job search, quickly became discouraged, and now sells water beds in Columbus, Ohio.

"Whether you're looking for your first or second job, the road trip is vital," says Rick Brown. "You've got to go on the road because news directors are getting deluged with resume materials every day. The road trip creates a relationship with the news director you can't get from a letter.

"Unless your tape absolutely bowls them over, you need to thrust yourself ahead of 90 percent of the people who have just sent tapes. You need to get to the station and meet the news director."

Little Rhyme or Reason

This is a strange and unpredictable business. While face-to-face contact is often beneficial, it's not always necessary.

When I left the Associated Press bureau in Hartford, Connecticut, my wife, Julie, and I moved back to Los Angeles. From there I sent out resumes, cover letters, and audition tapes and made a road trip in search of my first TV news reporting job. Knowing I'd have to start at the bottom, we thought we might as well try to live in one of the small markets in the Southwest, a little closer to our families and lifelong friends, and where sunshine is more plentiful.

Julie and I mapped out a ten-day road trip so that I could stop at just about every station in each small and medium market in California and Nevada, staying overnight with friends wherever possible, and taking advantage of a few cheap motels. While Julie worked in L.A.—someone had to pay the bills—I drove to the stations, hoping to meet the news directors to whom I had sent materials. I was able to set up a few interviews in advance and took my chances at the other stations.

In the end I had met with less than half the news directors I attempted to see, and usually only for a few minutes. Progress, nevertheless. I came close to getting a couple of jobs, but victory remained elusive. So I returned to L.A. to plan my next long drive, through Arizona and New Mexico.

Ironically, just a few days after returning from my first road trip, I was offered a job over the phone at a station in Yuma, Arizona. I had never even heard of the town before sending resume materials to a news director there. Yuma lies near the junction of Arizona's borders with California and Mexico. Because I was only about five hours away via car, I immediately drove to Yuma to see the KYEL-TV station and meet the staff before making a final decision, though I had little doubt I would take the job.

I guess the moral to this story is that there's no rhyme or reason in this business. It is possible to land a job solely by mail and telephone, although face-to-face contact made with news directors during road trips can stack the odds in your favor. I personally think it was just a fluke that the job I got in Yuma was at one of the few stations in the region I hadn't visited. Most of my friends in the business say personal interviews with news directors gave them an edge over other faces only seen on tapes.

Face-to-Face Success

"In the sports end of the business, everybody's tape tends to look pretty much the same," says Mark Olesh. "The thing I did differently that helped me clinch the sports job here was actually coming to the station to meet the news director. You have the chance to establish a rapport with the news director, which becomes even more important when you make subsequent calls to him. Just about everybody who works at this station got the job by coming through town to meet the news director."

"The most important thing is getting your face in the door," says Jodi Fleisig. "You've got to be able to sell yourself in person. Show how energetic, warm, and enthusiastic you are. That can even overcome a so-so audition tape. News directors will get excited about the fire in your belly. If you've got a good tape, not a great tape, you can still wow them in an interview.

"I knocked on so many doors, and once I got into the news director's office I sold myself. It's the only way to do it with all the competition out there. You've got to do something that makes you different."

▪13▪
The Interview

Doing Your Homework

Do a little market research before interviewing to find out what makes each town you've chosen tick. Is it an industrial or agricultural economy, or do most of its revenues come from tourism or the military? How big is the town? How and by whom is the city governed? Have any major news events occurred there recently?

News directors sometimes ask applicants what they know about the area, though they don't expect a dissertation. The more you know, the more likely you are to impress the news director, who'll see you're willing to go the extra mile.

"Do your homework," advises Lou Prato. "Students must have knowledge about the news business and the markets they're applying to."

You can get plenty of information by writing to a city's chamber of commerce or even by talking to members of the media in the area. If the news director isn't available to talk to you, as is often the case, leave a message. But go ahead and chat a little with the person on the other end of the line to learn a little more about the station and the city.

Questioning the Interviewer

Whether interviewing you in person or on the phone, news directors are likely to ask plenty of questions about your background. They may also be curious to know how you think news should be presented. But you, too, should ask questions. That's the job of a journalist. Find out as much as you can about the position for which you're applying and the philosophy of that particular news director. Try to determine whether he or she is the kind of leader under whom you'll enjoy working and grow professionally.

Keep in mind, however, that you must be willing to work for almost anyone, anywhere, in order to break in. If you're talented, motivated, and willing to learn, you probably won't be in that first job for more than a year or two anyway.

Take full advantage of what may be only a short time to sell yourself— to convey how you'd contribute to the news team. Without sounding too boastful, stress the highlights of your past experiences and how they've prepared you for the job. Lay it all on the line. You've got nothing to lose.

The Key for Assignment Editors

Interviews are important for everyone, but perhaps particularly so for assignment editors, who usually don't submit audition tapes.

"Assignment editors have to sell themselves first in the cover letter just to get an interview," says Jamie Avery, a former news director. "If they've sold me on the cover letter, then they have to sell themselves in person, in the interview.

"I'll want to find out how they would approach a news story, and what sidebars [other angles] can be looked into. You really can't just look at one news story as a single news story. There may be a bunch of other good story ideas there. News directors look for good news judgment, philosophy, imagination, and creativity.

"Also, it's important to find out about their experience with special projects, and how as assignment editors they'll handle breaking stories. It really is one of the most important jobs in the newsroom."

Avery thinks television news experience is helpful, but not necessary, for aspiring assignment editors. "You can teach people TV, but you can't teach them news," he says. "I'll take an assignment editor with newspaper experience any day. And news directors will often hire assignment editors locally. When I was in Harrisburg, I hired two assignment editors, both locally, one from radio and one from a newspaper. They both had news experience and good references.

"But sometimes a bright college intern can move up into that position and do a good job too," Avery adds.

Producer Talk and Tests

Like assignment editors, producers have a lot riding on their ability to sell themselves in an interview.

"News directors want to find out if the person has a strong enough personality to lead the news team and make the important decisions that producers have to make," says Rick Brown. "That can really come across only in an interview, and applicants should be ready to answer questions about that.

"News directors also want to make sure you're not just going to use the opportunity [the job as producer] to try to become a reporter and get on the air," he adds.

That, say many news directors, happens all too often, after they've spent a lot of time grooming someone for one of the station's top producer jobs.

Applicants for producer jobs may be asked to critique a particular newscast, often one produced at that station and overseen by the news director. It can be a show the news director liked, or one he or she didn't like. Talk about walking a tightrope! Sometimes a news director will use the technique to find out how much the applicant knows about producing news, and whether the interviewee's news philosophy is compatible with his or her own.

Jodi Fleisig suggests that applicants asked for such a critique look for the following elements, or lack thereof:

- Sharp, creative writing, with words matching video

- Stories flowing smoothly from one to the other

- Overall newscast moving at a healthy, even pace and holding viewers' attention

- Teases combining the best pictures and sharp writing to grab viewers and make sure they keep watching for the following stories

- Plenty of natural sound in the stories

- Friendly, professional anchors working well together

- Liveshots, or passed-up opportunities to do liveshots, from the scene of a story (if that station has the live-remote technology necessary for liveshots)

These elements should all look pretty familiar by now. They're all things producers must try to include on their audition tapes.

Just keep in mind that when asked to critique a given newscast, you may be evaluating the news director's favorite show or producer. So do the diplomatic thing: be honest, but refrain from overkill.

Testing Other Skills

Producers, reporters, and anyone else applying for a job that entails writing should be prepared to take a writing test. It doesn't happen too often, but some news directors interviewing applicants in person ask them to rewrite stories pulled from the wires, and to do so under deadline. Others have been known to actually send prospective reporters out to gather information on an unfolding story, then write and even edit a package on it.

Prospective photographers, too, may be sent into the field to do a little shooting, and videotape editors may be asked to "cut" (put together) a package.

Honesty *IS* the Best Policy

If you've been fired from another broadcasting job, don't lie about it or try to cover it up. Tell the news director why you were let go. Maybe it was budget cuts and you were the last hired. Maybe you made a mistake. Maybe your old boss just didn't like your work, or you.

Don't be afraid to tell what happened and what you learned from it.

The news director will be impressed with your honesty and will sense you're older and wiser from the experience. Many news directors have been laid off at one time or another themselves. It's far from a crime to be fired in this volatile business so dependent upon the ratings of the moment. It's the nature of the beast.

Dressing Like a Pro

When you interview in person, dress to impress. That's important for all candidates, but especially so if you plan to work on-camera. First impressions are crucial. You may not get a second chance. The news director will be imagining how you'd look on-camera and out in the community representing the station. That doesn't mean you have to wear an imported Italian suit. Just dress neatly, perhaps a bit conservatively, and be well-groomed.

▪14▪
Following Up

Staying in Touch

After establishing contact with news directors, whether in person, via phone, or by mail, stay in contact with them. Write thank-you letters to those who took time to see you or talk to you on the phone. Such a courteous gesture shows professionalism and can win you respect.

Even jot a note to the news directors who didn't make time for you. Include something like "I'm sorry we haven't had a chance to talk. But I'd certainly like to stay in contact in case any opportunities arise at your station and would greatly appreciate any advice you might render." You might even make those news directors feel a little guilty for not having made time for you. Maybe next time they will.

Check in with a news director every few weeks via phone and mail as a reminder of how eager you are to be part of the news team, and how hard you'd work if given the chance. With each letter you send, include a copy of your most current resume. The news director will likely get to know your name and background quite well. The idea is to make yours the first name that comes to mind when a job opens up. If the news director has already seen your audition tape or writing samples, and if you have access to TV news facilities, continue to send fresh material of which you're especially proud.

And whether you're looking for your first job or have already been in the business for a while, solicit feedback from news directors at the stations to which you're applying. Other than watching their newscasts, which isn't always possible, that's the only way to determine what they like and don't like. Some will be more cooperative than others. But they'll all appreciate your efforts to refine your skills.

There's nothing wrong with shooting for the stars. But make your job search a realistic one. Focus your energy and resources on stations where you truly believe you can get a start — probably not in a top 100 market if you're looking for your first job on-camera, but maybe so for photographers, assignment editors, researchers, writers, and producers, depending on other experience, professional contacts, and luck.

Chin Up

Don't get discouraged. Everyone in this business, no matter how talented, must learn to cope with rejection, especially considering the popularity of TV news and the great number of people competing for each job. Keep at it. *Persistence* will pay off in the long run.

"Even in the best of circumstances, it can take a long time to get your first TV news job," says Rick Brown. "You've got to be patient. And not only you. Your family must also be patient. They may not understand how tough this business is. You need to explain to them that it's not like being lawyers or doctors who are almost guaranteed a job when they get out of school.

"A job search of one to ten months is to be expected. I've seen very talented people go six, seven, eight months before being given an opportunity to prove themselves. And many of them have gone on to fantastic careers. You've just got to stay with it."

∎ 15 ∎
On the Job

Once you've landed a job, don't slack off! Work hard. Make the most of that job by fulfilling and stretching your responsibilities, gaining valuable experience at every turn. While your first couple of jobs aren't likely to pay much, the hard work will help you move up the ladder toward a better-paying position in a larger market.

Pushing It to the Limit

Working at small stations gives you the chance to learn, refine your skills, and even experiment with new ideas. Take full advantage of that. The standards and expectations aren't quite as high as at larger news organizations, and there's less pressure to perform flawlessly.

Cultivate a good working relationship with your news director and fellow staff. They can provide you with the tips and constructive criticism essential for growth. Also, take time to observe how the other networks and local stations combine their pictures, natural sound, and narration to tell news stories.

Watch carefully and learn from the pros. Let them take you under their wing. Solicit their advice and listen closely. Study their writing, reporting, shooting, and editing techniques. You'll find there are plenty of rules of thumb upon which to build your career. But developing your own style just may be the quickest way to succeed in the ever-evolving TV news business.

■16■
Salaries: A Dose of Cold Reality

The Great Divide

The following statistical information just might separate those who really want to be television journalists from those only looking to make themselves a fast fortune. If you fall into the journalist category, read on.

If you perform your job well and are willing to hang in there for the long haul, sufficient financial rewards will likely follow. But at the entry level, starting salaries are extremely low—sometimes less than $12,000 a year in the smallest markets. Small TV stations usually can't afford to pay much, nor do they have to with so many people competing for jobs. (Many do, however, offer decent benefits packages, including major medical coverage.)

Vital Stats

A study published in the February 1992 issue of *Communicator* reveals a great deal about TV news salaries. Based on information from 506 commercial TV stations responding to a survey, Vernon Stone found that the salaries of most TV news employees have failed to keep up with the rise in the cost of living. Some have even dropped.

"Salaries stood still last year for many broadcast journalists," wrote Stone. "Overall nationally, median pay in mid-1991 was roughly the same as in mid-1990 for TV reporters, producers, anchors and news directors. . . . The cost of living increased nearly 5% in the same period.

"Pay levels were generally up at TV network affiliates in the 50 largest markets on average, but unchanged or down in other markets."

Stone continued: "Typical [median] salary levels in TV news outpaced the cost of living only for executive producers, who averaged a $2,000 increase. . . . Rank and file producers and reporters showed no gain. Neither did news directors. Photographers, assignment editors and assistant news directors posted gains that lagged the CPI [Consumer Price Index, or cost of living]. Median pay for anchorpersons was down slightly from 1990.

"TV news pay for most positions increased in the East and stood still in the South, Midwest and West.

"Average anchorpersons in every market category were making less last year than in 1990—12% less at ADI [market size] 1–25 network affiliates, 6% less at ADI 1–25 indies [independent stations] and 1–2% less in other markets.

"But star anchors, the highest paid at their stations, beat the cost of living at network affiliates in ADI 1–25 (up 16%) and stations in the ADI 26–50 (+5%) and ADI 151–208 (+7%) categories. It is evident that few star anchors in major markets took pay cuts, as was being talked. . . .

"Median pay for star anchors went up 4% in ADI 101–150, down 8% in ADI 51–100 and down 27% at ADI 1–25 indies.

"Reporters' salary medians increased 15% at ADI 1–25 network affiliates, 16% in ADI 26–50 and 2% in ADI 51–100. They were down 12% at ADI 1–25 indies, down 4% in ADI 101–150 and flat in ADI 151–208.

"Producers bettered the cost of living at ADI 1–25 network affiliates, and ADI 26–50 stations, lost ground at indies and either held their own or gained less than the CPI elsewhere.

"Photographers beat the CPI in ADI 1–50, held their own in ADI 51–100 and lost slightly in smaller markets.

"Assignment editors' median salaries fell 2%–5% in various market categories.

"Assistant NDs [news directors] stayed ahead of the CPI at ADI 1–25 network affiliates, gained but trailed the CPI in ADI 26–100 and lost ground elsewhere.

"TV news directors saw their median salaries rise 5% at ADI 1–25 network affiliates and 4% in ADI 26–50, fall 5% at ADI 1–25 indies and 4% in ADI 26–50, and stand still in ADI 51–100 and ADI 151–208."

From his research, Stone concluded that the gap has widened between the highest-paid broadcast journalists and the vast majority of others:

"Thousands of broadcast newspeople took cuts in purchasing power last year. For the most part, salary levels either rose less than the cost of living, went unchanged or even dropped.

"Some moved ahead, most notably news directors and star anchors at large TV operations in major markets. They were already the highest paid.

"But the workhorses of TV news—the rank and file reporters, anchors and producers—tended to find little if any change in their paychecks."

The following charts break down median TV news salaries by market size and job title and show whether average salaries have risen, remained flat, or dropped. It's important to remember that in each job category, some employees earn considerably less money than average and some earn more. The precise amount of money one makes depends largely on experience, the size of a station and its news staff, and the financial health of that station.

Table 2

Median TV News Salaries by Market Size, Full-Time Staff, and Region, 1991

	Typical ENG Cam	Typical Producer	Exec Producer	Typical Reporter	Typical Anchor	High Anchor	Assign Editor	Asst. ND	News Director	N
ADI 1–25	$35,000	$34,860	$55,000	$47,750	$ 80,000	$183,750	$35,000	$67,500	$ 90,000	60
Net Affils	$39,625	$40,000	$61,875	$57,000	$107,000	$232,500	$39,200	$76,700	$105,000	37
Independents	$25,000	$29,000	$37,000	$26,500	$ 47,000	$ 53,500	$27,500	$47,000	$ 50,000	23
ADI 26–50	$24,500	$27,250	$41,500	$30,500	$ 59,200	$102,500	$30,500	$47,500	$ 67,500	41
ADI 51–100	$18,000	$21,325	$30,500	$21,000	$ 38,975	$ 55,000	$27,500	$35,650	$ 50,000	114
ADI 101–150	$15,000	$17,665	$23,000	$16,320	$ 27,600	$ 36,500	$20,600	$29,500	$ 36,500	83
ADI 151–208	$13,290	$15,250	$20,675	$15,050	$ 21,200	$ 30,000	$17,500	$21,270	$ 32,000	54
Staff 0–10	$13,950	$17,000	$19,050	$15,150	$ 18,465	$ 22,650	$16,700	$22,650	$ 26,800	52
Staff 11–20	$14,500	$17,750	$21,000	$16,100	$ 24,700	$ 34,000	$18,500	$23,790	$ 36,000	97
Staff 21–35	$17,490	$21,000	$30,500	$21,000	$ 37,500	$ 61,000	$26,500	$36,650	$ 48,965	116
Staff 36–180	$27,425	$29,900	$45,000	$35,500	$ 72,500	$135,000	$33,000	$57,285	$ 81,065	86
East	$20,500	$24,000	$45,000	$22,500	$ 34,500	$ 60,000	$29,375	$47,500	$ 45,500	59
South	$16,500	$20,335	$31,000	$19,000	$ 35,000	$ 50,500	$25,000	$34,000	$ 46,000	110
Midwest	$17,500	$21,000	$31,250	$19,125	$ 33,000	$ 50,000	$26,175	$39,800	$ 40,800	102
West	$19,500	$24,500	$38,000	$20,000	$ 34,500	$ 50,000	$27,800	$41,000	$ 43,250	82

Source: Vernon Stone, Communicator, Feb. 1992.

Table 3

Annual TV News Salaries in 1991 and Change from 1990

	All Stations		Net Affiliates		Independents	
	Median	Mean	Median	Mean	Median	Mean
Camerapersons	$17,800	$21,400	$17,500	$21,135	$20,000	$23,755
	+2.6%	+4.6%	+2.9%	+6.3%	.0%	−1.0%
Producers	$21,000	$24,260	$21,300	$23,660	$23,500	$29,585
	.0%	+4.2%	+2.4%	+3.8%	−12.1%	+7.8%
Exec Producer	$34,000	$37,750	$33,500	$37,550	$35,000	$40,120
	+6.2%	+4.3%	+4.7%	+5.2%	−2.8%	+6.3%
Reporters	$20,000	$25,485	$19,500	$25,405	$24,250	$26,790
	.0%	+1.9%	.0%	+4.3%	−18.5%	−13.9%
Anchors	$34,500	$48,600	$35,000	$49,070	$35,000	$46,000
	−1.4%	−4.8%	.0%	−3.4%	−11.9%	−13.6%
High Anchor	$49,500	$82,835	$50,000	$86,005	$47,500	$53,250
	−1.0%	+3.0%	.0%	+6.4%	−9.7%	−30.3%
Assignment Ed	$26,000	$27,815	$26,000	$27,860	$26,500	$27,495
	+1.5%	+.1%	+3.9%	+2.1%	+11.3%	+5.0%
Assistant ND	$39,500	$43,845	$39,600	$44,115	$38,500	$41,455
	+1.9%	+3.3%	+4.3%	+4.7%	−3.8%	−9.1%
News Director	$45,000	$51,745	$45,100	$52,760	$39,000	$44,745
	.0%	+2.2%	+.2%	+4.2%	−6.6%	+12.0%
N for NDs	339		297		40	

Source: Vernon Stone, Communicator, Feb. 1992.

Note: Independents tend to be in larger markets.

■17■
Toughen Up!

The competition is incredibly fierce at all levels of TV news. Job seekers compete for a foot in the door. Members of a news team compete against each other for choice assignments, though the level of in-house rivalry varies greatly. And stations battle it out for scoops and ratings points.

Despite all that competition, some of it cutthroat, good ratings are usually the result of teamwork, with television journalists cooperating to fulfill the goals of the station's news management. Personal ambitions and achievements, while important, must remain secondary.

News Nomads

The highs derived from breaking stories, winning awards, and helping the station attain strong ratings are great. Nothing is more rewarding. But one must also brace for the lows of the business. Poor ratings and a change in news management, for example, can mean an end to your job and a move to another city. "Cleaning house" is the term used in the business to describe situations in which much of the news team is let go and replaced in one fell swoop.

"One of the things you have to understand about it is that it's an unstable, volatile business," says Marv Rockford. "That's probably not of much concern to a lot of people who've just gotten out of college when they're 21 or 22 years old. But 15 years down the road, if you're married, and you have children, and your spouse has a career and a job, and you get fired or just fed up with the place you're working for, it isn't like you can just easily switch to another accounting firm, or go to another law firm. Generally, if you want to stay in news, there are only two or three other places in town where you can be employed, and the number of jobs at those stations is quite limited. You just might have to move.

"So if you don't have the appetite to be in an unstable career where it's a very performance-driven, what-have-you-done-for-me-today kind of existence, then television news is probably not the career for you," Rockford continues. "If you're not prepared to make a lot of moves, four, or five moves in the first ten years — you might be better off doing something else."

However, while the process of moving is always a pain, experiencing life in different parts of the country can be great fun. My wife and I have thoroughly enjoyed exploring the several different regions in which we've lived.

Thickening Your Skin

Moving and stiff competition on the job pose physical and mental challenges one must learn to handle. But there's emotional pressure too—pressure to perform well, every day of the week.

"Also, you get feedback on your work, positive or negative, all the time," says Michael Eskridge. "So you have to develop a kind of thick skin because you're constantly being judged.

"But there's something about television news that a lot of other jobs don't have. You prepare a story. You put it on the air. It goes out over the airwaves. People see it. They'll say something about it — that it's good, bad, or indifferent. But the bottom line is it's over. It's not something that requires years of planning and of which you'll never see the end result."   That is true. Every day brings results — win or lose. And each day we try again.

■18■
Watch Your Mouth

Whenever speaking into or even just working near a microphone, whether in the field or at the station, assume that mike is "hot"—picking up every word you say. Derogatory remarks or foul language can come back to haunt you in many ways.

Learning from a Costly Mistake

The following is a true story I hesitate to tell for fear it will embarrass a reporter I know. But nothing in my experience better illustrates how cautious broadcasters must be around microphones.

While I was working at KYEL-TV in Yuma, this man was hired as a part-time reporter/part-time photographer. After only a few weeks at the station, he was in an editing room recording his narration to a story he'd just finished writing. He stumbled during the first sentence and loudly exclaimed a couple of four-letter words. No big deal, right? But instead of rewinding the tape and recording over his error, the reporter simply laid another video countdown on the tape and started again.

When the reporter finished the package, he cued the tape to the appropriate second countdown. The story aired during our noon newscast and

125

everything went fine. But, later, one of the young tape operators at the station, failing to pay close attention to things, rewound the tape too far, back to the first countdown—the one that preceded the two infamous words. The stage for disaster was set.

During the six-o'clock newscast that evening, the anchors introduced the reporter's story. The director rolled the tape. As soon as he realized there was only black following the countdown, he cut away from the tape back to the anchors on the set. The audio, however, remained on for a few seconds, and the reporter's mistake was transmitted into the living rooms of thousands of loyal viewers, many of them watching with their children.

What made the incident even worse was that the anchors on the set hadn't heard the tape and were laughing about something else when the director cut back to a shot of them. To the viewers it looked as though they were laughing about what had just happened. That only added fuel to the fire.

Needless to say, the phones in the newsroom began to ring, and ring, and ring. People were furious. Unfortunately, I was still working in the newsroom during the broadcast and ended up answering some of those calls.

"Please tell me that I didn't hear what I think I heard just now on your station," said one irate woman. "My whole family was sitting around the dinner table and watching your newscast as we always do. And I just can't believe it!"

What could I say? "Lady, you're just imagining things. Go back to dinner!"? No, and neither could the station deny responsibility.

So less than four hours later, at the top of the ten-o'clock newscast, our station's news director broadcast a formal apology for what had happened. He assured viewers that the station took the mistake every bit as seriously as they did, and that action was being taken to make sure it wouldn't happen again.

Sure enough, the reporter was fired first thing the next morning. The tape engineer who had miscued the tape received a three-day suspension.

Such foul language can contribute to the loss of a station's broadcasting license, let alone destroy a station's ratings—particularly in a small, conservative town. For those reasons most stations won't tolerate that kind of mistake, not even once. And with so many qualified candidates out there looking for jobs, a news director need only pick up the phone to quickly find a replacement.

To be sure, similar exclamations of choice profanity and obscene hand gestures have been conveyed over the airwaves (there are plenty of such bloopers floating around the business) by well-known reporters and anchors who didn't know they were being recorded, or simply didn't care. But their jobs, however, are usually far more secure, mainly due to their following and revenue-producing power. Although some stations and major networks have overlooked such mistakes, they maintain that offensive utterances or actions are inexcusable.

In this particular case the reporter showed little remorse. As a matter of fact, he even denied at first that he had used foul language. And he later stated to members of the news staff, "It could have happened to anybody." Personally, I would have been on my knees on the newsroom floor, apologizing profusely, and begging senior management for forgiveness. As you know by now, such jobs aren't easy to find.

▪19▪
Ethics

The RTNDA provides a strong philosophical foundation for broadcast journalists with the following Code of Broadcast News Ethics.

The responsibility of radio and television journalists is to gather and report information of importance and interest to the public accurately, honestly and impartially.

The members of the Radio-Television News Directors Association accept these standards and will:

1. Strive to present the source or nature of broadcast news material in a way that is balanced, accurate and fair.

    A. They will evaluate information solely on its merits as news, rejecting sensationalism or misleading emphasis in any form.

    B. They will guard against using audio or video material in a way that deceives the audience.

    C. They will not mislead the public by presenting as spontaneous news any material which is staged or rehearsed.

    D. They will identify people by race, creed, nationality or prior status only when it is relevant.

E. They will clearly label opinion and commentary.

F. They will promptly acknowledge and correct errors.

2. Strive to conduct themselves in a manner that protects them from conflicts of interest, real or perceived. They will decline gifts or favors which would influence or appear to influence their judgments.

3. Respect the dignity, privacy and well-being of people with whom they deal.

4. Recognize the need to protect confidential sources. They will promise confidentiality only with the intention of keeping that promise.

5. Respect everyone's right to a fair trial.

6. Broadcast the private transmissions of other broadcasters only with permission.

7. Actively encourage observance of this Code by all journalists, whether members of the Radio-Television News Directors Association or not.

Personal Rewards

One of my most personally rewarding experiences as a journalist came after I left my TV news reporting job in Yuma. Several weeks after arriving in Colorado Springs, I received a letter from Rick Pavey, a leader of the Republican Party in Yuma. Pavey had helped me line up one-on-one interviews with Keith DeGreen, the Republican candidate who was trying to unseat Democratic U.S. Senator Dennis DeConcini in the 1988 campaign. Someone who knew me quite well let it slip to Pavey during a casual conversation that my own political views tend to be quite liberal.

In his letter Pavey wrote: "Jeff, I was told you are a pretty solid Democrat. To a Democrat from a Republican, I want to thank you for your unbiased coverage of the Keith DeGreen campaign that I worked on. Every time I called for an interview or to give you news you were accommodating and very fair in your coverage and for that I thank you very much."

I found that letter incredibly rewarding. It acknowledged my efforts to put aside my own opinions as I portrayed each candidate's arguments on important issues and the charges they leveled against each other.

Striving for Objectivity

Complete objectivity is merely a myth. No matter how dispassionate the reporter, it's impossible to remain 100 percent objective 100 percent of the time. Every journalist brings certain preconceived notions and biases into each story.

In her book *And So It Goes*, TV journalist Linda Ellerbee writes: "Any reporter who tells you he's objective is lying to you. 'Objective' is impossible; . . . there is no such thing as a reporter who comes to a story able to forget everything he's ever heard, seen or had happen to him."

But the desire to achieve objectivity remains paramount. Journalists must struggle to keep their own views from seeping into stories. They must strive to examine all sides and angles of an issue. Accurately reporting facts and the different ways that information is perceived gives the viewer an opportunity to draw his or her own conclusions.

That doesn't mean reporters shouldn't follow their gut instincts. It's the journalist's job to dig relentlessly below the obvious facts, public record, and official comments to expose the true nature of issues. That kind of probing goes well beyond the all-too-frequent level of mediocrity and can result in outstanding, revealing stories.

We live in an age of well-rehearsed news conferences designed by various groups and politicians to manipulate the media and slant the coverage. All the more reason for journalists to look beyond that which the particular group or person allows to be seen or heard. As in a thrilling murder mystery, true motives must be uncovered and disclosed.

Often, seemingly mundane issues can lead to fascinating stories. Who in the world was interested in the nation's troubled savings and loan institutions until a handful of reporters uncovered the depth of corruption involved, and the hundreds of billions of dollars it would cost taxpayers to bail out the S & L's?

The Watergate scandal provides another example of the need for, and success of, such investigative reporting. In this case journalists dug deeply to expose the lies and distortions communicated by high-ranking government officials trying to deceive the public. Their efforts dramatically swayed public opinion and paved the road for a more critical approach to news reporting at all levels—international, national, and local.

Investigative journalism is an integral part of democracy because it keeps the most powerful elements of society in check. And in this day and age when a majority of people rely on television as their primary source of news, it's the job of TV journalists not only to dig deep for facts and perspective but to present that information in compelling ways that trigger contemplation about the world in which we live. After all, a well-informed public is best able to govern itself wisely.

A Final Note

Keep in mind that just as there's no single way of presenting TV news, there's no one way to go after a job in the business. Each person's background and application materials are different. I've merely tried to lay out the rules of thumb and plenty of options. In the end you must do what *feels* right. If you have your own ideas, give them a whirl.

Persevere! Good Luck! And happy hunting!

Appendix

Resources for Undergraduate and Graduate Broadcast Journalism Programs and Scholarships

President, Broadcast Education Association
National Association of Broadcasters
1771 N Street, N.W.
Washington, DC 20036
(202) 429-5355

Radio-Television News Directors Association
1717 K Street, N.W.
Washington, DC 20006
(202) 659-6510

National Executive Secretary
National Broadcasting Society, AERho
College of Journalism
University of South Carolina
Columbia, SC 29208

Details on all Television Stations (Broadcast and Cable)

Broadcasting & Cable Market Place
1705 DeSales Street, N.W.
Washington, DC 20036
(202) 659-2340

Television and Cable Factbook
2115 Ward Court, N.W.
Washington, DC 20037
(202) 872-9200

Bibliography

Writing News for Broadcast by Edward Bliss, Jr., and John M. Patterson, Columbia University Press, 1978.

Writing Broadcast News—Shorter, Sharper, Stronger by Mervin Block, Bonus Books, 1989.

Rewriting Network News: WordWatching Tips from 345 TV and Radio Scripts by Mervin Block, Bonus Books, 1990.

TV News Off-camera: An Insider's Guide to Newswriting and Newspeople by Steven Zousmer, Univ. of Michigan Press, 1987.

Voice as an Instrument by Raymond Rizzo, Macmillan, 1978.

Broadcast Voice Handbook: How to Polish Your On-air Delivery by Ann Utterback, Bonus Books, 1990.

ENG: Television News and the New Technology by Richard Yoakam and Charles Cremer, S. Illinois Univ. Press, 1989.

Basic TV Reporting: Media Manuals by Ivor Yorke, Focal Press, 1990.

Interviews that Work: A Practical Guide for Journalists by Shirley Biagi, Wedsworth, 1986.

VGM CAREER BOOKS

OPPORTUNITIES IN
Available in both paperback and hardbound editions

Accounting
Acting
Advertising
Aerospace
Agriculture
Airline
Animal and Pet Care
Architecture
Automotive Service
Banking
Beauty Culture
Biological Sciences
Biotechnology
Book Publishing
Broadcasting
Building Construction Trades
Business Communication
Business Management
Cable Television
Carpentry
Chemical Engineering
Chemistry
Child Care
Chiropractic Health Care
Civil Engineering
Cleaning Service
Commercial Art and Graphic Design
Computer Aided Design and Computer Aided Mfg.
Computer Maintenance
Computer Science
Counseling & Development
Crafts
Culinary
Customer Service
Dance
Data Processing
Dental Care
Direct Marketing
Drafting
Electrical Trades
Electronic and Electrical Engineering
Electronics
Energy
Engineering
Engineering Technology
Environmental
Eye Care
Fashion
Fast Food
Federal Government
Film
Financial
Fire Protection Services
Fitness
Food Services
Foreign Language
Forestry
Gerontology
Government Service
Graphic Communications
Health and Medical
High Tech
Home Economics
Hospital Administration
Hotel & Motel Management
Human Resources Management Careers
Information Systems
Insurance
Interior Design
International Business
Journalism
Laser Technology
Law

Law Enforcement and Criminal Justice
Library and Information Science
Machine Trades
Magazine Publishing
Management
Marine & Maritime
Marketing
Materials Science
Mechanical Engineering
Medical Technology
Metalworking
Microelectronics
Military
Modeling
Music
Newspaper Publishing
Nursing
Nutrition
Occupational Therapy
Office Occupations
Opticianry
Optometry
Packaging Science
Paralegal Careers
Paramedical Careers
Part-time & Summer Jobs
Performing Arts
Petroleum
Pharmacy
Photography
Physical Therapy
Physician
Plastics
Plumbing & Pipe Fitting
Podiatric Medicine
Postal Service
Printing
Property Management
Psychiatry
Psychology
Public Health
Public Relations
Purchasing
Real Estate
Recreation and Leisure
Refrigeration and Air Conditioning
Religious Service
Restaurant
Retailing
Robotics
Sales
Sales & Marketing
Secretarial
Securities
Social Science
Social Work
Speech-Language Pathology
Sports & Athletics
Sports Medicine
State and Local Government
Teaching
Technical Communications
Telecommunications
Television and Video
Theatrical Design & Production
Transportation
Travel
Trucking
Veterinary Medicine
Visual Arts
Vocational and Technical
Warehousing
Waste Management
Welding
Word Processing
Writing
Your Own Service Business

CAREERS IN
Accounting; Advertising; Business; Communications; Computers; Education; Engineering; Health Care; High Tech; Law; Marketing; Medicine; Science

CAREER DIRECTORIES
Careers Encyclopedia
Dictionary of Occupational Titles
Occupational Outlook Handbook

CAREER PLANNING
Admissions Guide to Selective Business Schools
Career Planning and Development for College Students and Recent Graduates
Careers Checklists
Careers for Animal Lovers
Careers for Bookworms
Careers for Culture Lovers
Careers for Foreign Language Aficionados
Careers for Good Samaritans
Careers for Gourmets
Careers for Nature Lovers
Careers for Numbers Crunchers
Careers for Sports Nuts
Careers for Travel Buffs
Guide to Basic Resume Writing
Handbook of Business and Management Careers
Handbook of Health Care Careers
Handbook of Scientific and Technical Careers
How to Change Your Career
How to Choose the Right Career
How to Get and Keep Your First Job
How to Get into the Right Law School
How to Get People to Do Things Your Way
How to Have a Winning Job Interview
How to Land a Better Job
How to Make the Right Career Moves
How to Market Your College Degree
How to Prepare a Curriculum Vitae
How to Prepare for College
How to Run Your Own Home Business
How to Succeed in Collge
How to Succeed in High School
How to Write a Winning Resume
Joyce Lain Kennedy's Career Book
Planning Your Career of Tomorrow
Planning Your College Education
Planning Your Military Career
Planning Your Young Child's Education
Resumes for Advertising Careers
Resumes for College Students & Recent Graduates
Resumes for Communications Careers
Resumes for Education Careers
Resumes for High School Graduates
Resumes for High Tech Careers
Resumes for Sales and Marketing Careers
Successful Interviewing for College Seniors

SURVIVAL GUIDES
Dropping Out or Hanging In
High School Survival Guide
College Survival Guide

VGM Career Horizons
a division of *NTC Publishing Group*
4255 West Touhy Avenue
Lincolnwood, Illinois 60646-1975